Contents

CHAPTER

What This Book Is About

Sales promotion has become a big, big business in the United States. In 1980, for example, U.S. marketers invested about $49 billion in sales promotion,[1] up 15 percent from the previous year. These figures now put sales promotion investments well ahead of media expenditures by marketers.

To get some idea of how important and how pervasive sales promotion has become, consider these facts:

- Today over 90 billion cents-off coupons are distributed in the United States—more than 400 coupons for each man, woman, and child in the country.
- The typical home now receives more than 500 direct mail offers each year.
- To lure shoppers, the typical large supermarket builds or installs more than 2,500 product displays each year.
- Marketers now invest more than $640 million annually in self-liquidating premiums.
- The number of cents-off packs offered to retailers by manufacturers doubled in the most recent four-year measurement.
- The print media are carrying more and more sales promotion events and advertising in their pages. In a single issue of one women's magazine, 23 separate advertisements featuring some sort of sales promotion event appeared. More than 31 premium and sweepstake events alone were counted in just 17 recent issues of women's magazines.

---

[1] Russell D. Bowman, "MC's 2nd Annual Report on Advertising and Promotion Expenditures" *Marketing Communications*, August 1981, pp. 43 *et seq.*

There's no question about it: sales promotion is big business—and getting bigger. But despite the size and growth of the industry, there is little information about it that is readily available to the interested student or beginner in the field.

On the following pages you'll find descriptions and illustrations of sound, practical, well-established, and proven sales promotion techniques and how they can be mixed and matched to fit a specific situation and achieve the best results. You will see exactly how and why a particular sales promotion technique works, and you will see the importance of integrating advertising and sales promotion to optimize return on investment. In addition, the sales promotion organizations, suppliers, and other experts listed at the back of the book can help answer many questions.

Twelve Basic Sales Promotion Techniques

We believe that all sales promotion can be reduced to 12 basic and fairly simple techniques. While there may be many variations, all modern sales promotion plans use one or more of these 12 basic tools:

- Coupons
- Contests or sweepstakes
- Bonus packs
- Stamp and continuity plans
- Price-offs
- In-packs, on-packs, near-packs, and reusable containers
- Free-in-the-mail premiums
- Self-liquidating premiums
- Refund offers
- Trade coupons
- Trade allowances
- Sampling

The list is short, and you may think you have seen many more sales promotion ideas. You most likely have, but consider that these 12 basic sales promotion techniques can be combined to offer 823,-059,745 different approaches. And that doesn't include all the different ways creative layout and copy can present these techniques to the consumer. With so many alternatives, the difficulty of choosing and combining them might seem a bit overwhelming. To do so, you must understand the criteria for choosing the right technique for a particular situation or to solve a particular marketing problem. Each technique has reasonably well-defined strengths and weaknesses. The job of the sales promotion manager, therefore, is to combine the strengths and compensate for the weaknesses. In most cases a combination of two (or more) techniques will give better results than either technique used alone. That's called synergism, and it's what makes successful promotions.

But you must know the strengths and weaknesses of each of these 12 sales promotion tools to know how to select the winning combination. That's what you'll find in this text. For example,

- If you want people to read your advertising, offer them an incentive. One of the best attention-getters is a sweepstakes, a technique that gets people emotionally involved in the advertising and builds readership.
- If you want to increase redemption of a coupon or an offer, add a sweepstakes to the promotion. You'll get a higher rate of return on your coupon.
- If you want to get more action at the retail level, offer a coupon and promote it to the trade. We've found that retailers are more likely to buy more of the product, build their inventories, and give off-shelf displays if a coupon is part of the promotion than through any of the other techniques available.
- If you want to build response to a couponing program at the retail level, add a trade contest. That usually builds sales volume higher than just a consumer promotion alone.

These are only a few ideas that can be drawn from analyzing the 12 basic sales promotion techniques covered in this book. Study their various advantages and disadvantages and learn from the experience of marketers who have tried and tested them. You can then proceed confidently and with a reasonable expectation of success in your own sales promotion efforts.

Coupons

Couponing is one of the most widely used and most effective sales promotion techniques. Traditionally, coupons have been thought of as certificates that entitle the holder to a price reduction, a special value, or a gift of some sort for making a purchase. More recently, coupons have been used to provide all sorts of incentives to the customer, from refunds to combination offers and even free samples of the product. While they can be used in many ways, coupons seem to work best in sales promotion programs designed to help a product or service that is not living up to its sales or profit expectations. For example, coupons can be used

- To reverse an overall decline in sales in the product or service category. They cannot, however, reverse a downward trend over several years.
- To increase a declining share for the particular brand in the total category.
- To stir up interest in a brand with static sales in a growing category.
- To help a brand with a declining margin despite sales that are steady or growing in the category.
- Coupons can generate product trial.

The number of coupons distributed in the United States has been increasing dramatically, as a Nielsen Clearing House study demonstrates. (See Table 2-1.) A more recent study shows that more than 90 billion manufacturer-originated coupons were distributed in 1980, up 12 percent since 1979. And the figures will probably continue to increase each year. In addition, the number of households using coupons is also growing fast. Table 2-2 illustrates the growth in coupon users over a five-year period. The figure was 76 percent in 1980 and is likely higher today.

5

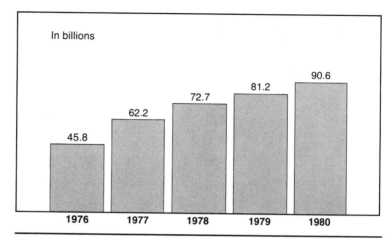

TABLE 2-1. Trend in Coupon Distributions (in billions)
Source: Richard H. Aycrigg, "Coupon Distribution and Redemption
Patterns," *NCH Reporter* (Northbrook, IL: A. C. Nielsen Co., 1981), p. 3.

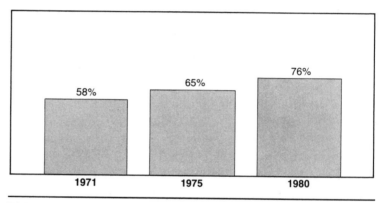

TABLE 2-2. Percent of Households Using Coupons
Source: Aycrigg, "Coupon Distribution and Redemption Patterns," p. 3.

One of the most noticeable changes in coupons has been increasing face value. For years, coupon values were in the 7¢ to 10¢
range. Now it is not unusual to see coupons with face values of 25¢,
50¢, or even $1 or more on a fairly wide range of products. The
average coupon value on grocery-store products is now over 18.5¢,
according to A. C. Nielsen Company. Coupon values also vary by
type of distribution, as illustrated in Table 2-3.

Coupons seem to work best with older, better educated, urban
married couples. They seem to be less effective with young, single,
less educated, less affluent customers. This doesn't mean that cou-

	Newspaper Coupons	Sunday Supplement Coupons	Free-Standing Insert Coupons	Magazine Coupons	Direct Mail Coupons	In/On Pack Coupons	Total Distributions (All Media Combined)
Average Face Value	15.0¢	16.2¢	14.7¢	14.2¢	17.1¢	13.0¢	14.9¢
Face Value/Percent 100%	7¢/9%	7¢/13%	7¢/6%	7¢/12%	7¢/8%	7¢/17%	7¢/11%
	10¢/36%	10¢/31%	10¢/48%	10¢/42%	10¢/22%	10¢/45%	10¢/39%
	12¢/4%	12¢/4%	12¢/7%	12¢/3%	12¢/4%	12¢/3%	12¢/4%
	15¢/25%	15¢/23%	15¢/19%	15¢/22%	15¢/29%	15¢/18%	15¢/23%
	20¢/10%	20¢/10%	20¢/8%	20¢/11%	20¢/14%	20¢/8%	20¢/10%
	25¢/11%	25¢/12%	25¢/9%	25¢/7%	25¢/17%	25¢/6%	25¢/9%
	30¢+/5%	30¢+/7%	30¢+/3%	30¢+/3%	30¢+/6%	30¢+/3%	30¢+/4%

TABLE 2-3. Percent of Coupon Distribution by Face Value within Media
Source: Aycrigg, "Coupon Distribution and Redemption Patterns," p. 7.

pons will or won't work with either of these groups; it simply means that on the average the redemption of coupons is not as high with the second group as it is with the first. Coupons also seem to appeal to some ethnic groups more than others, although there is less definitive information on this.

Types

There are two kinds of coupons: (1) trade-originated and (2) manufacturer-originated. Trade-originated coupons are redeemable only at a particular store or group of stores. Usually, they are developed by a wholesaler or retailer and appear in their print advertisements, in in-store flyers, or at the point-of-purchase. The objective of most trade-originated coupons is more to encourage the consumer to shop at a particular store than to purchase a particular brand. They are also widely used to help build impulse purchases of individual items within a store. In many instances, trade-originated coupons are a cooperative venture between the retailer and the manufacturer of the product. Their goal is to offer an incentive both to shop the particular store and to purchase a particular brand as well. See Chapter 11 for a discussion of trade coupons.

Manufacturer-originated coupons are developed and distributed by the maker or the marketer of the product. They are usually redeemable at the point-of-purchase and good for a price reduction or special value on the purchase of the product. With manufacturer-originated coupons, the retailer acts as the agent for the manufacturer. That is, the retailer accepts the coupon and returns it to the manufacturer through some sort of "clearing house" arrangement. Then the retailer is reimbursed for the face value of the coupon, plus a handling charge. Manufacturer-originated coupons may be used at any participating retailer that handles the product or brand.

To simplify things, we'll devote the rest of this chapter to a discussion of manufacturer-originated coupons, of which there are four types—distinguished primarily by the method of distribution. They are: (1) direct-to-consumer, (2) media-distributed, (3) merchandise-distributed, and (4) specialty-distributed coupons.

Direct-to-Consumer Coupons

This type of coupon is usually distributed door-to-door or through some form of postal or delivery service, directly into the hands of the consumer. In either case, coupons may be delivered singly or as part of a group. They can also be distributed on street corners by demonstrators, at displays, through store-shelf "take one" pads, on transit systems, and by other "direct to the consumer" methods.

There are several advantages to direct coupon distribution. First, you can be very selective with the target market. For example, you can select groups from high-income zip codes, by sex or employment, or on the basis of other demographic features. This type of couponing is more efficient on a cost-per-trier basis than sampling. Second, you can be fairly confident of the rate of return. About 60 percent of the homes that receive direct mail coupons actually use them. Third, relatively low duplication is possible. By mailing directly to the home, you can reach nearly 90 percent of all the households in the U.S. Fourth, this type of coupon distribution is also fairly well accepted by the consumer, the trade, and the sales force. Coupons distributed by direct mail have higher redemption rates and get about three times as many new product triers as can be achieved through magazine distribution. Major disadvantages are the extremely high delivery costs and the threat of misredemption or theft.[1]

The cost of developing a direct mail coupon drop includes the coupon itself, the mailing list, postage, envelopes, stuffing, and addressing, plus the redemption costs and the clearing house charges

---

[1]Sales Promotion Committee, American Association of Advertising Agencies, *Sales Promotion Techniques: A Basic Guidebook* (New York: American Association of Advertising Agencies, 1978), p. 14.

for coupons used by recipients. Because distribution costs have risen so dramatically in the past, many advertisers are now turning to co-op mailings. These are mailings of coupons organized by an outside group or by several noncompetitive advertisers who distribute their coupons together and split the cost. An example of the former is the Carol Wright program developed by Donnelley Marketing.

The cost of door-to-door delivery of coupons is almost prohibitive for many advertisers simply because of the price of labor to distribute them. While this type of couponing is still practiced in some areas, it is almost nonexistent in many major urban markets. A typical door-to-door delivered coupon sample and premium is the one for Dynamo detergent in Figure 2-1. This coupon was distributed along with a sample of the product and other information. The package was hung on the doors of homes in many areas.

FIGURE 2-1. Door-to-door Coupon

The Total cereal coupon (Figure 2-2) is typical of the direct mail form of distribution. It was mailed with several others in a co-op mailing by Publisher's Clearing House. The coupon was part of a folder that contained a sales message for the product.

Figure 2-3 illustrates some of the coupons from a Carol Wright mailing. This co-op mailing is conducted several times each year. Donnelley Marketing gathers the coupons, develops a mailing list,

FIGURE 2-2. Direct Mail Coupon
Source: Courtesy of General Mills, Inc.

FIGURE 2-3. Co-op Mailing Coupon
Source: Photo courtesy Donnelley Marketing.

and actually posts the coupons in a single envelope. Either the manufacturers furnish Donnelley with the required number of coupons to be inserted in the ensemble or Donnelley prints them to specifications.

Media-Distributed Coupons

The second major type of coupon distribution method is through the media. This includes coupons appearing in newspapers, magazines, Sunday supplements, or other print media. Within these media vehicles are several coupon variations.

Newspapers Newspaper-distributed coupons can be either solo (Figure 2-4) or multiple (Figure 2-5). Solo coupons are those that are included in an advertisement for a single advertiser, such as the one for Kellogg's Corn Flakes, or the advertisement may contain coupons for several brands, such as those illustrated in Figure 2-5.

In this case, all the coupons are for brands by a single manufacturer. Co-op coupons, on the other hand, are from a group of non-competitive manufacturers who have either joined together or been gathered together by another organization to distribute coupons. All are placed under a common heading and run together. The coupons get the benefit of large space display, and each coupon tends to help draw consumers to the others. A co-op coupon ad developed by Newspaper Co-Op Company with multiple sponsors is shown in Figure 2-5.

There are several advantages to newspaper-delivered coupons. First, they are fairly low in cost; only the cost of the newspaper space and some production costs are involved. For example, the cost to deliver a newspaper coupon in a 1,000 line, black and white size to newspaper subscribers in U.S. cities with populations of 50,000 or more was about $5 per thousand in 1979. Second, some selectivity is possible, based on the choice of newspaper in each community, although the density of newspaper distribution in the area selected may be a limitation. Third, newspaper coupons are quite flexible in terms of size, shape, timing, and location of distribution. Fourth, there are opportunities to tie-in with newspaper features, such as Best Food Days or sports pages. Fifth, because of the short newspaper lead time, coupons can be inserted and distributed quite rapidly. Newspapers also have the broadest urban reach and the fastest rate of redemption.

There are also disadvantages to this method of distribution. Redemption rates and efficiency on a cost-per-redeemer basis are low. The newspaper may have poor reproduction of the material because of the newsprint. Fraudulent redemption and duplication by thieves are much easier. In addition, the coupon may well be "lost" among

FIGURE 2-4. Newspaper Coupon

the multitude of other coupons and offers appearing in that particular edition.[2]

Magazines Magazine coupons are usually of the on-page or pop-up variety. "On-page" simply means that the coupon appears within a regular advertisement for a marketer, usually on the regular printed page of the publication. An example of an on-page coupon that appeared in *Reader's Digest* for Mega Vitamins is shown in Figure 2-6. The "pop-up" is a coupon that appears as a separate card next to or attached to the regular advertisement. It is usually

---

[2]*Sales Promotion Techniques*, p. 15.

FIGURE 2-5. Co-op Newspaper Coupon
Source: Courtesy of Newspaper Co-op.

FIGURE 2-6. On-page Magazine Coupon
Source: Courtesy of J. B. Williams Co. and Parkson Advertising Agency.

on heavier stock than the magazine, smaller in size, and bound or tipped into the publication. Because of its method of insertion, the coupon literally "pops up" when the reader reaches it. It works, too, since pop-up coupon redemption is about 60 percent greater than on-page coupon redemption. An example of a pop-up coupon for Ecotrin Analgesic is illustrated in Figure 2-7.

Magazines offer many advantages. Coupon delivery cost is low, particularly for the on-page type. The coupon itself can be specifically tailored to the magazine's readers. Reasonable area selectivity

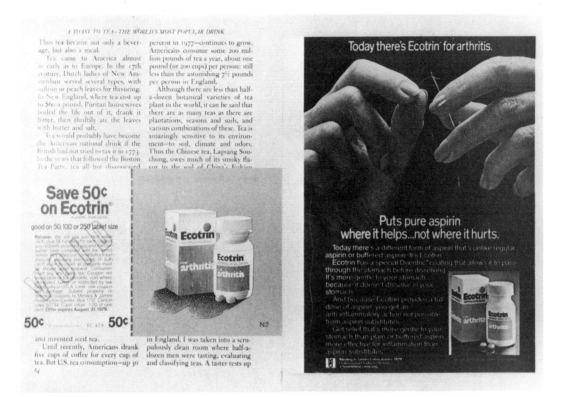

FIGURE 2-7. Pop-up Magazine Coupon
Source: Courtesy Menley & James Laboratories.

is possible through regional and other special editions of many magazines. A major advantage is the higher reproduction quality magazines offer over other print media, particularly newspapers.

Of course, there are disadvantages. First, it is virtually impossible to reach more than 60 percent of U.S. households without major duplication problems. Therefore, unless the magazine list is carefully selected, one prospect may receive several coupons. Second, most magazines have long lead times, which require that the promotion be planned and executed far in advance. Third, the lack of geographic distribution flexibility makes many magazines difficult to use for some marketers.

In terms of coupon delivery costs, magazines are quite reasonable. For example, in 1979 the cost of general weekly and women's magazines averaged about $5 per thousand circulation for a full-page, four-color advertisement in which a coupon could be carried. An additional charge of $7 to $9 per thousand would have been required for the use of a pop-up coupon either bound or tipped in.[3]

Sunday Supplements Sunday supplement coupons come in two kinds. The first, the regular coupon, usually appears as part of a regular advertisement printed in the magazine section or attached to the page in some way. The second, the "free-standing insert," is most often a separate page or section on which advertising and various coupons have been printed. These inserts are not printed as part of the regular newspaper or supplement section. Rather, they are preprinted and inserted in the edition along with the comics, the magazine section, or other magazine section features. They are said to be "free-standing" since they are not attached to the newspaper in any way.

Free-standing inserts are of two types: those for individual advertisers and those developed as cooperative ventures. Individual advertiser inserts contain advertising copy and coupons for only one advertiser or marketer. Cooperative inserts usually involve a number of noncompetitive advertisers who have either joined together to share the cost of the insert or have been organized by an outside firm that provides this service. In either case, the cost of developing and printing the insert and the charges for newspaper space are shared on a proportionate basis.

Coupons appearing as a part of a regular newspaper Sunday supplement section and printed by the newspaper are billed at the normal newspaper space rate for that section. Free-standing inserts, however, are usually billed by the newspaper at a cost-per-thousand rate based on the circulation. In addition, since the advertisers furnish the inserts to the newspaper ready to place in the paper, the costs of printing and shipping them to the newspaper for distribution are over and above the actual space charges. Figure 2-8 illustrates a free-standing "impact" insert developed by Valassis Newspaper Marketing Corporation.

The advantages and disadvantages of the Sunday supplement as a coupon carrier are the same as those for magazines. Coupons in the Sunday supplement do get higher redemption than daily newspapers. The cost, however, is somewhat higher than that of magazines. For example, a full-page, four-color advertisement in Sunday supplements cost approximately $5.75 per thousand in 1979, based on charges quoted by major market newspapers.

Free-standing inserts are quite a different matter. They are highly flexible; they can be used wherever and whenever a newspaper will accept them. And the advertiser can be very selective in their distribution. Furthermore, inserts are generally considered to be

---

[3]*Sales Promotion Techniques*, p. 16.

FIGURE 2-8. Free-standing Sunday Supplement Coupon
Source: Reproduced courtesy of General Foods Corp., owner of the registered trademark Brim.

more cost-efficient than direct mail. And they have higher redemption rates. They can also be targeted to specific groups or markets through distribution methods and creative appeals.

There are also disadvantages to inserts. They can easily be lost, stolen, or misredeemed since they are detachable from the publication. In some cases, poor insertion practices by newspapers and magazines mean that all circulation areas are not always covered. Also, it is often difficult to get insertion dates for inserts. Many publications limit the number of inserts they will accept on a given date or have certain dates or issues for which they will accept none. Since inserts must be printed in advance and shipped to the newspaper or magazine, a long lead time is required. Finally, the cost of paper and printing of the inserts is an additional cost not found in on-page insertions.

Merchandise-Distributed Coupons

Merchandise-distributed coupons are those distributed with the product and are usually good on the next purchase. They are often described as being "in-packed" or "on-packed." An in-pack is simply a coupon that has been included within the product package. The coupon is usually placed in the box or carton with a "flag" on the outside calling attention to it. Special care must be taken with in-pack coupons, particularly if they are to be included in food products. There are often quite stringent Food and Drug Administration restrictions on how and in what form the coupon may be placed in the box, and there may be certain paper and printing requirements as well. An example of an in-pack coupon "flagged" on the package is illustrated in Figure 2-9 for Life cereal.

An alternative to the in-pack is the on-pack coupon. This simply means that the coupon is attached to the package in some way. The coupon could be part of the wrapper or even printed as a part of the carton itself. An example of an on-pack coupon for Coffee-mate nondairy creamer from Carnation is shown in Figure 2-10. The coupon is actually the back side of the wrap-around label on the jar.

Finally, a coupon for one product may be placed either in or on another unlike product. This is called a "cross-ruff." Often, this is done for products that go together naturally. For example, a brand of coffee might in-pack or on-pack a coupon good for a nondairy creamer, or a lunch meat package might carry a coupon redeemable on cheese, and so on. In some instances, these cross-ruffs are developed by combining various products owned by the same company, or they may involve separate companies. For example, Arrid wanted to generate high levels of displays and features for its antiperspirant. Cross-Ruff Clearing House organized a partnership promotion for Arrid with 10 other brands. Store coupons (Figure 2-11) for the 10 other brands, totaling $1.55 in value, were packed under the Arrid caps, which were colored gold for the occasion. Thus, Arrid provided distribution of the coupons for the other products while the coupons gave Arrid an extra value to the trade and the consumer. To add further impact and emphasis to the promotion theme, a Solid Gold sweepstakes was added. In this way, all brands in the promotion benefited.

The major advantage of an in-packed or on-packed coupon is that

FIGURE 2-9. In-Pack Coupon
Source: Courtesy The Quaker Oats Company.

there is practically no distribution cost. The product itself carries the coupon. The "flag" on the front panel also provides a point of difference at the point-of-purchase for the product and the coupon. An additional advantage is the mimimum coupon waste, since only purchasers receive coupons. While in- or on-pack coupons tend to reward present users rather than generate new triers, there is high redemption potential. And since the manufacturer controls the distribution of the product, it is possible to control the areas of distribution and thus the potential consumers who receive the coupon. Finally, cross-ruffs offer excellent opportunities to distribute coupons to new users or to new groups of prospects through noncompetitive products.

On the other hand, in- or on-pack coupons attract few new triers; they tend only to reward present users. In some instances, special

FIGURE 2-10. On-Pack Coupon
Source: Courtesy of Carnation Company.

equipment or materials may be required to either insert or print the coupons on the package, thus increasing the costs. Also, the coupon offered is usually on the *next* purchase, not the one being made now. And the coupons are confined to stores in which the product is available. Finally, in-pack coupons may be overlooked by consumers, and on-pack coupons may be difficult for the consumer to remove from the package.

There is no standard way to estimate the cost of either in-pack, on-pack, or cross-ruff coupons since the primary cost is for printing and inserting the coupons in or on the package. This may vary widely. Production or packaging people for the specific brands are usually the best ones to estimate the cost of such a couponing program. In addition to the cost of preparation, you must, of course, always include the cost of estimated redemption when budgeting for any type of coupon.[4] But remember that in- and on-pack coupon redemptions are usually much higher than coupons distributed through the media, as the Nielsen Clearing House study in Table 2-4 shows.

Specialty-Distributed Coupons

A small, but apparently growing number of ways to distribute coupons can now be found, particularly at the retail level. These include techniques such as coupons printed on the back of cash register tapes, on grocery bags (Figure 2-12), on egg cartons, on frozen foods, and the like. Uniqueness is the major claimed advan-

---

[4]*Sales Promotion Techniques*, pp. 18–19.

FIGURE 2-11. Cross-Ruff Coupon
Source: A Cross Ruff Clearing House Promotion.

tage of coupon distribution methods such as these, but that can also
be a disadvantage. Since many of these techniques are fairly new
and have short track records, they should be viewed with caution.
Costs are so varied that it is impossible to even suggest any guidelines. We can only recommend that you evaluate the cost of these
specialty coupon distribution techniques against more established
methods. While some may appear to be better values, close investigation often shows that the more traditional methods are more suc-

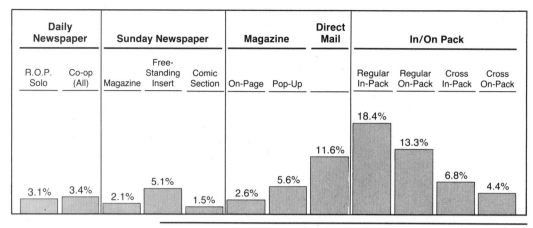

Daily Newspaper		Sunday Newspaper			Magazine		Direct Mail	In/On Pack			
R.O.P. Solo	Co-op (All)	Magazine	Free-Standing Insert	Comic Section	On-Page	Pop-Up		Regular In-Pack	Regular On-Pack	Cross In-Pack	Cross On-Pack
3.1%	3.4%	2.1%	5.1%	1.5%	2.6%	5.6%	11.6%	18.4%	13.3%	6.8%	4.4%

TABLE 2-4. Coupon Redemption Rates by Media

Source: Aycrigg, "Coupon Distribution and Redemption Patterns," p. 5.

cessful. (A very important type of coupon, the trade or in-ad coupon, will be covered in Chapter 11 under Trade Coupons.)

Table 2-5, a chart developed by Nielsen Clearing House, gives a comparison of the number of manufacturer-originated coupons distributed over a three-year period by distribution method. From this, you can see that daily newspapers carried the largest number of coupons, more than 48 percent of the total, followed by free-standing inserts and magazines. Also, you'll notice that there were some definite changes in the overall percentage carried by each medium during the measured time.

The Advantages

Besides the special advantages that pertain to each type of coupon, there are also advantages to couponing in general, regardless of the type, value, or method of distribution:

1. Coupons can be used to obtain trial of a product, whether it is new or established. It is estimated, for example, that 65 percent of all coupon redeemers are new users of the product. That ranges from up to 100 percent for new brands down to 50 percent for established brands. It should be noted, however, that using couponing to induce trial is usually more expensive than other available techniques. K. C. Blair has estimated that the cost of gaining a new customer for an established product using cents-off coupons ranges from a high of $27.17 in some categories to a low of $1.96 in others.[5]

---

[5]Louis J. Haugh, "Will High Cost of Couponing Force More Product Samples?" *Advertising Age*, March 6, 1978, p. 56.

FIGURE 2-12. Shopping Bag Coupon

Source: Courtesy of Dominick's Finer Foods, operators of 70 high-quality, high-volume supermarkets in the Chicago-land area.

Therefore, you should use coupons to induce trial with some caution.

2. Coupons can be used to convert brand triers into regular users. The use of a price reduction, such as a coupon, on a product that has been tried and found acceptable can be most effective. Coupons offer a method of offering the extra incentive to purchase. This is particularly true in parity product categories.

	TOTAL	100%	100%	100%
Daily Newspaper — R.O.P. Solo		40.2%	36.2%	31.1%
Daily Newspaper — Co-op (All)		15.4	16.1	17.1
Sunday Paper		7.7	9.5	9.0
Sunday Fr.-St. Insert		13.4	14.9	18.4
Magazine / Direct Mail		11.4	12.2	13.3
		3.0	3.2	3.4
In/On Pack		8.9	7.9	7.7
		1978	1979	1980

TABLE 2-5. Percent of Distributions by Media
Source: Aycrigg, "Coupon Distribution and Redemption Patterns," p. 3.

3. Coupons can be used to reach a large number of prospects or participants quickly. Usually, couponing is more efficient than other forms of sales promotion, such as sampling, particularly when the objective is to achieve trial. Because coupons can usually be redeemed at multiple retail locations, several distribution systems can be used. In addition, coupons can be targeted to specific groups of consumers through the use of various specialized media vehicles.

4. Coupons can help load regular users. As a method of offsetting competitive actions, coupons can be used as an incentive for regular customers to purchase more of the couponed brand than normal. This "loading up" often takes customers out of the market for a period of time and decreases the effectiveness of competitive activities.

5. Coupons can be used to introduce a new flavor, size, or other line extension of the product. When the product is known or accepted, coupons can be an effective way to encourage present users to try a new size, a new flavor, a new package, or another form of the product. A reduced price made available by a coupon is usually an effective method of generating sales.

6. Coupons can be used to help trade the consumer up to a larger or more expensive size of the product. When the consumer is at the shelf, a coupon can help justify the extra cost of a more expensive product or can encourage the purchase of a larger size. It's often just the extra "push" needed to make the sale.

7. Coupons are generally used fairly quickly by consumers. Compared to other forms of sales promotion, the pull-through of coupons is good. While returns may drag on for several

months, depending on the method of distribution, studies have shown that the majority of the redemptions of cents-off coupons occurs within the first four months. (See Tables 2-6, 2-7, and 2-8.)

8. Coupons can help increase trade purchases. When retailers know a coupon is to be distributed, they are usually more willing to stock up on the product to cover the expected increase in consumer buying.

9. Coupons are an effective selling tool for the sales force. The

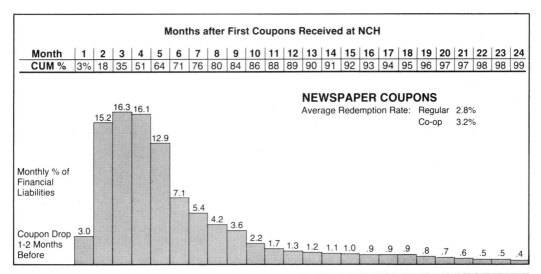

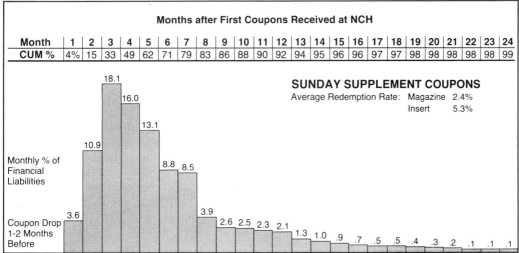

TABLE 2-6. Redemption Rates: Newspaper and Sunday Supplement Coupons

Source: Aycrigg, "Coupon Distribution and Redemption Patterns," p. 15.

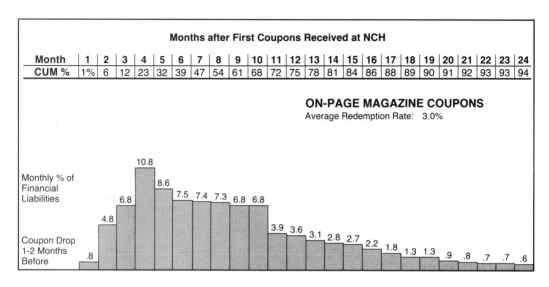

Month	1	2	3	4	5	6	7	8	9	10	11	12	13	14	15	16	17	18	19	20	21	22	23	24
CUM %	1%	6	12	23	32	39	47	54	61	68	72	75	78	81	84	86	88	89	90	91	92	93	93	94

Months after First Coupons Received at NCH

ON-PAGE MAGAZINE COUPONS
Average Redemption Rate: 3.0%

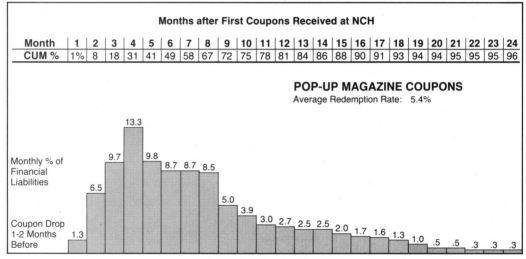

Month	1	2	3	4	5	6	7	8	9	10	11	12	13	14	15	16	17	18	19	20	21	22	23	24
CUM %	1%	8	18	31	41	49	58	67	72	75	78	81	84	86	88	90	91	93	94	94	95	95	95	96

Months after First Coupons Received at NCH

POP-UP MAGAZINE COUPONS
Average Redemption Rate: 5.4%

TABLE 2-7. Redemption Rates: Magazine Coupons
Source: Aycrigg, "Coupon Distribution and Redemption Patterns," p. 16.

announcement of a forthcoming coupon drop usually generates additional effort by the manufacturer's sales force. It also gives them a competitive edge in selling to retailers.

The Disadvantages

While we've painted a bright picture of what coupons can do, there are also some disadvantages:

1. Misredemption is a serious problem. The misredemption of coupons either intentionally as fraud or through oversights on

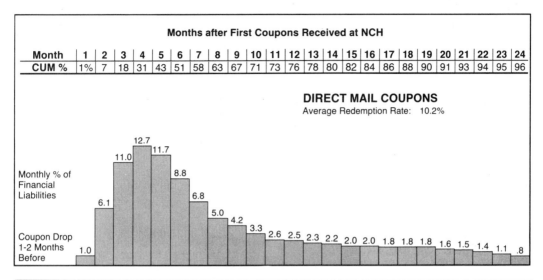

Month	1	2	3	4	5	6	7	8	9	10	11	12	13	14	15	16	17	18	19	20	21	22	23	24
CUM %	1%	7	18	31	43	51	58	63	67	71	73	76	78	80	82	84	86	88	90	91	93	94	95	96

Months after First Coupons Received at NCH

DIRECT MAIL COUPONS
Average Redemption Rate: 10.2%

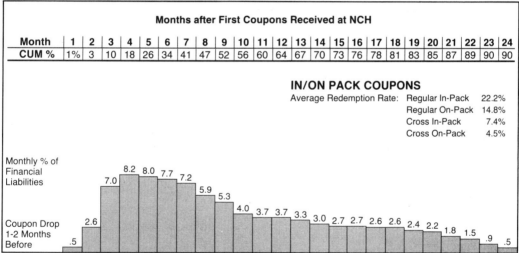

Month	1	2	3	4	5	6	7	8	9	10	11	12	13	14	15	16	17	18	19	20	21	22	23	24
CUM %	1%	3	10	18	26	34	41	47	52	56	60	64	67	70	73	76	78	81	83	85	87	89	90	90

Months after First Coupons Received at NCH

IN/ON PACK COUPONS
Average Redemption Rate: Regular In-Pack 22.2%
Regular On-Pack 14.8%
Cross In-Pack   7.4%
Cross On-Pack   4.5%

TABLE 2-8. Redemption Rates: Direct Mail and In/On-Pack Coupons
Source: Aycrigg, "Coupon Distribution and Redemption Patterns," p. 17.

the part of the consumer or the retailer is an increasingly serious and costly problem. (More on this later in this chapter.)

2. Response is unpredictable. Problems in allowing sufficient budget for redemption are often created because of lack of information on results. Such factors as face value, timing, brand share, distribution, creative approach, competitive activities, and media selection all combine to make an estimate

of the total number of redeemed coupons hard to judge. This makes financial responsibility difficult to determine in advance.

3. Some coupons can take a long time to redeem. As we illustrated in the previous section, most types of coupons redeem fairly quickly, but they can drag out over time. Thus, reserves must be held to protect against future redemptions. Although not a major problem, unanticipated costs may arise long after the coupons have appeared. Adequate provisions must be made to cover this contingency.

4. Coupons are most effective during and just before the product's peak selling season. While this might appear to be an advantage, it may not be. During this period, good sales for the product are expected. So, to be effective, coupons must build new or additional sales in off-seasons, too.

5. Coupons don't work as well for new or unknown products or services. Consumers apparently judge coupon value on the amount of reduced price against a known or established product. Therefore, coupons don't seem to be as effective for products with an unknown value or for which a certain standard of quality has not been established. A "saving" is not necessarily considered important unless the "comparable price or value" is known.

Some Guidelines

Even with all this information about the different types of coupons, their methods of distribution, and their advantages and disadvantages, it is still possible to misuse them as a sales promotion technique. As we show in the following pages, it is important to design coupons carefully, in both form and content. It is also necessary to estimate redemption, avoid misredemption, and calculate costs.

The Message

While coupons may be of any size or shape, advertisers usually try to make them the size and shape of a dollar bill. This makes them easier for the consumer, the retailer, and the clearing house to handle. While there are no specific physical requirements for a coupon, the cardinal rule is: *If it is a coupon, make it look like a coupon.* It is senseless to confuse or discourage coupon use with clever lettering or cute sayings. While the coupon should be tied to the theme of the promotion, its message should be loud and clear; the "arts and crafts" can be added later.

An important part of the coupon is what is called the "boiler-plate," or the details of the offer. This is simply the copy that explains the coupon to both the consumer and the retailer. There are some fairly standard formats for this material. It may appear on

FIGURE 2-13. Coupon: Front and "Boilerplate"
Source: Reprinted by permission of The Clorox Company.

either the front or the back of the coupon, depending on the size and type available. The Clorox 2 coupon is a good example of how to present the message clearly and completely. The size is 5¼ × 2½ inches, both sides are printed in full color. The front features the coupon offer and value, the back gives the details. The coupon looks valuable, makes the offer boldly and clearly, expressly states the limitations of the coupon, and has a bit of selling copy to help encourage use. You should particularly notice the copy on the back of the coupon, outlining the details of the offer. It is quite clear, and the expiration date is contained at the end of the statement. This placement of the expiration date can help prevent retailer misredemption after the coupon has expired since it is easily seen and read.

Coupon Redemption

One of the great uncertainties of sales promotion is the rate at which product coupons will be redeemed. While averages have been determined, there are always the "unusual" ones that go against the norm. Since coupon redemption costs are the major factor in a sales promotion program of this type, it is unfortunate that we can't be more confident of our predictions. As it is, we're forced to use norms, "rules of thumb," and previous experience as guides.

While the newspaper is the leading coupon carrier, in-pack and on-pack coupons are redeemed 6 to 10 times more often than newspaper coupons. But the method of distribution is only one factor in coupon redemption. There are several others. For example, the size of the individual product class in the retail store's volume, i.e., the rate of sale of the product class or category per $1,000 of the store's all-commodity volume, has a great influence on coupon redemption rates. Most studies have shown that the higher the product class sales in the store, the higher the redemption rate of coupons in that category. Thus, a product that accounts for $6 out of each $1,000 (.6 percent) of sales in the store usually redeems 30 percent better than a coupon on a product that accounts for only $2 of each $1,000 (.2 percent) in sales and 300 percent better than one with less than $1 of each $1,000 in sales. Another factor that influences redemption is the rate of discount of the coupon offer, i.e., the amount of the value of the coupon compared to the selling price of the product. The actual coupon value also has much to do with the rate of redemption. Most studies have shown that a 30 percent discount off the retail price is the optimal coupon value; that is, it brings the best redemption.[6] Items with a fast turnover redeem at higher rates, and the higher the discount rate of the coupon face value, the greater the redemption.

Distribution of the product seems to have a great effect on coupon redemption, too. A brand with 90 percent distribution gets double the redemption of a brand with 50 percent distribution. Surprisingly, the actual share of the market for the product appears to have very little effect. Competitive activity and degree of product familiarity also have little influence on coupon redemption.

In summary, Nielsen Clearing House found that 13 major factors influence the redemption of coupons.

1. Method of distribution
2. Product class size
3. Audience reached by coupon
4. Consumer's "need" for product
5. Brand's consumer franchise
6. Degree of brand loyalty
7. Brand's retail availability
8. Face value of coupon
9. Whether new or old brand
10. Design and appeal of coupon ad

---

[6]*Sales Promotion Techniques*, p. 19.

11. Discount offered by coupon
12. Area of country
13. Competitive activity[7]

Coupon Misredemption

Redemption is important, but so is misredemption. Unfortunately, this problem is growing. Although there are no complete figures on what rate or value of misredemption really occurs, a study by K. C. Blair showed that consumer misredemption of coupons ranged from a high of 54 percent to a low of 14 percent, with an average of 33 percent. On the other hand a study by Manufacturer's Marketing Services estimated consumer misredemption at only about 3 percent. Whatever the rate, misredemption is a serious problem. None of these figures includes misredemption by theft rings, which often operate across the country. These are usually groups or organizations that cut coupons wholesale from newspapers or magazines. They may also duplicate them or simply steal them and redeem them through unscrupulous merchants.[8] Care should be taken to insure as much as possible against misredemption by careful coupon planning and implementation. Remember, coupons are money.

Just how important a problem is misredemption of coupons? Although there are no firm figures, estimates of misredemption by medium have been developed by Donnelley Marketing and are shown in Table 2-9.

With coupon misredemption estimated as high as 45 percent in some media, every attempt to control coupon redemption is not only desirable but necessary. American Marketing Corporation developed the following suggestions to help minimize misredemption:

- Treat coupons as money.
- Discourage bulk redemptions through design, distribution, and handling.
- Don't use excessive values in coupons. Keep them within reason.
- The coupon value should not exceed the cost of the media in which it is distributed or the value of the product if it is a solo coupon.
- Keep the offer clear and uncomplicated. Cute or clever approaches make it more difficult for the retailer to understand the offer.

---

[7]Richard H. Aycrigg, "Current Couponing Trends," given at *PMAA Promotion Forum*, New York, N.Y., March 1, 1979.
[8]Haugh, "Will High Cost of Couponing Force More Product Samples?" p. 56.

Type of Distribution	Extent of Fraudulent Misredemption
Magazines	
On-page	8 – 10%
Pop-up	12 – 15%
Newspaper	
ROP Co-Op	25 – 30%
ROP-Best Food Day	20 – 25%
Free Standing Insert	30 – 45%
Sunday Supplement	12 – 15%
Direct Mail	
Co-Op	0 – 1%
Solo	0 – 1%
Product Package	
In-pack	0 – 1%
On-pack	0 – 1%
Instant redeemable	8 – 10%
Other	
Handout-sales	15 – 20%
Coupon w/sample	3 – 5%

TABLE 2-9. Estimated Misredemption of Coupons
Source: Courtesy of Donnelley Marketing.

- Have no less than 50 percent product distribution in the area in which the coupon will be distributed.
- Make it easy for the retailer to handle the coupon and to be repaid.
- Set a policy and stick to it. Don't hesitate to refuse payment for redemptions that are clearly fraudulent.
- Test your programs and methods to educate the consumer. Don't go national or even regional without some sort of test to make sure the coupon works.[9]

In addition to the above list, one primary rule applies: make your coupons difficult to duplicate or counterfeit. With today's sophisticated copying machines, one of the easiest ways to misredeem coupons is simply through duplication and gang cutting. One of the best ways to halt this practice is to use four-color coupons. Unless the coupon value is extremely high, it simply doesn't pay the criminal to reproduce coupons in color.

In summary, coupon misredemption is a serious problem, and everything possible should be done to attempt to reduce it.

---

[9]Louis J. Haugh, from a speech given to the American Marketing Corporation, for *Advertising Age*, 1979.

A Special Note on Costs

There are two types of costs connected with coupons: those involved with distribution and those involved with redemption. Distribution costs are incurred in getting the coupons to the consumer such as printing, media costs, and postage. Redemption costs are associated with the payment and allocation of the discount to the consumer, the retailer, and any middlemen.

Redemption costs normally consist of the value of the coupon, or the amount listed as the face value of the coupon and the various costs of redeeming it. Normally, in addition to the discount they give the consumer, retailers are allowed a set price per coupon they redeem. Currently, that is 7¢ per coupon, which is paid to the retailer by the manufacturer or distributor of the coupon. Because of the volume of coupons, retailers simply cannot return them to each manufacturer for payment. Middlemen organizations—clearing houses—have thus sprung up. Retailers forward the coupons to the clearing house, which then .pays the retailer the face value plus the retailer handling charge. These clearing houses then separate the coupons and bill each manufacturer for the coupons which they receive or "clear." For this service, the manufacturer pays a fee to the clearing house. At this time, the fee is approximately 3½¢ per coupon. A. C. Nielsen Company operates one of the largest of these clearing houses.

Costs

The calculation of coupon return costs is relatively easy. You simply collect all the actual or potential costs and add them up. An example will illustrate.

Assume that you have placed an advertisement in the local newspaper containing a coupon worth 15¢ off on the next purchase of your product. You want to estimate the cost of that coupon. Let's say that the newspaper space cost is $1,000 and the circulation is 100,000. If you expect the normal coupon redemption rate for a regular newspaper advertisement, what would the estimated cost of the coupon be?

First, you must include the cost of the newspaper ad space, that is, $1,000. Further assume that the production of the ad is $250 (the cost of layout, type, plates, etc., necessary to place the ad in the newspaper). You therefore have a total investment of $1,250 before you calculate coupon redemption costs.

Next, you estimate that your coupon will be redeemed at a normal rate for regular newspapers, or about 2.8 percent of the newspaper's circulation. Based on a circulation of 100,000, you can then estimate that approximately 2,800 coupons will be redeemed (100,-000 × 0.028). The cost of those 2,800 coupons will be:

2,800 coupons at face value of 15¢	$420
+ 7¢ to dealer for handling	196
+ 3½¢ for postage and clearing house costs	98
	$714

Circulation Method	Cost per M Printing Delivery	Average Redemption	Distribution Cost (1)	Total Number of Redemptions	Redemption Costs (2)	Total Program Cost	Cost per Coupon Redeemed
DIRECT MAIL							
Co-Op	$14	10.2%	$350,000	2,555,000	$485,450	$835,450	32.6¢
MAGAZINE							
Solo	6	3	150,000	750,000	142,500	292,500	39 ¢
Page plus pop-up	12	5.4	300,000	1,350,000	256,500	556,500	41.2¢
NEWSPAPER							
Solo r.o.p.	3.75	2.8	93,750	700,000	133,000	226,750	32.4¢
Co-op r.o.p.	1	3.2	25,000	800,000	152,000	177,000	22.1¢
SUNDAY SUPPS.							
Solo	6	2.4	150,000	600,000	114,000	264,000	44 ¢
Free-standing inserts	2.25	5.3	56,250	1,325,000	251,175	307,425	23.2¢

(1) Distribution cost based on 25,000,000 circulation; some programs have more, others less distribution. Also, rates vary with circulation selection.
(2) Redemption costs based on 14¢ face value plus 5¢ handling charge and 1¢ international handling charge.

TABLE 2-10   Cost per Coupon Redeemed Based on Redemption Rate
Source: Louis J. Haugh, "MCA, with 11% Share, Leads in Co-op Coupon Delivery," *Advertising Age*, June 13,1977, p. 71.

In this case, the cost per coupon redeemed is not the 15¢ face value but 25½¢ each, or a total of $714 for the 2,800 you estimate will be redeemed. If you include the cost of the space to carry the coupon, $1,000 plus $1,250 for the preparation and production of the advertisement, the total cost of the coupon promotion will be $1,964. On this basis, for the estimated 2,800 coupons you expect to be redeemed, the average cost will be about 70¢ each. If your coupons are redeemed at a rate higher than 2.8 percent of course your costs will be higher but the cost per coupon will be lower.

The same approach can be used to estimate redemption costs for any type of coupon. You may use the redemption estimate charts in Table 2-6 to calculate coupon returns. However, to be on the safe side, you should always allow a bit higher figure than the estimated rates. Remember, these are averages and subject to wide fluctuations in either direction.

Another way of looking at the cost of coupon redemption is to evaluate it on the basis of costs by various methods of distribution. The chart shown in Table 2-10 was developed by Louis J. Haugh to illustrate the differences in redemption rates among various media. It is interesting to note how different the costs are, based on the distribution methods.

FIGURE 2-14. A $1,000 Coupon
Source: Courtesy AGS Computers, Inc.

One of the most interesting uses of coupons we have seen is illustrated in Figure 2-14. As you can see, this is actually a coupon for $1,000 that can be redeemed by persons answering the ad (and employed by AGS Computers, Inc.) after 30 days. What a sales promotion idea and what a way to make an offer stand out on a crowded employment page!

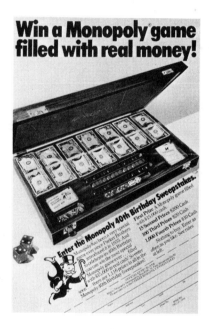

Contests and Sweepstakes

Probably the most exciting and potentially rewarding sales promotion devices for the consumer are contests and sweepstakes. Over the years, marketers have offered almost every imaginable prize or reward to the winners of these events, ranging from thousands of pounds of the product to gold, silver, and precious jewels. In fact, some marketers have offered hundreds of different prizes in an attempt to draw consumers to their promotion.

While contests and sweepstakes can be successful in many sales promotion situations, they seem to work particularly well when the product or brand is not living up to its sales or profit goals or expectations. While this problem can be caused by many factors, its solution may sometimes be quite simple: the marketing effort for the brand needs a shot in the arm to stimulate sales. Contests and sweepstakes can provide the extra incentive that is needed to get sales or profits moving again.

Experience shows that few sales promotion events can create as much excitement in the market as a well-planned and well-executed contest or sweepstakes. Either can be used not only to build consumer interest but also to inspire the sales force. Surprisingly, even the trade, particularly retailers, react well to this type of promotion. They seem to like the excitement and involvement that a contest or sweepstakes can bring to the retail store.

Perhaps one of the most important features of a contest or sweepstakes promotion is the opportunity to make the event seem much larger than it really is in terms of the amount of money invested. For example, several trips to Europe or a half-dozen new cars can provide a large prize package to winners that looks much more impressive than the same amount spent in samples or cents-off coupons. In addition to all this excitement, there is ample evidence that solid sales promotion objectives and sales gains can be achieved through a well-organized contest or sweepstakes.

In the late 1960s and early 1970s, contests and sweepstakes were changed considerably because of an investigation conducted by the federal government. The investigation was based on the suspicion that some contests and sweepstakes at the time were misleading or even fraudulent. Some marketers were listing a large number of prizes but awarding only a small portion of them. The usual explanation was that "preselected winning entries" did not claim the prizes. As a result of the investigation, several changes were made in the rules for conducting contests and sweepstakes. These rules are now quite strict and complex. For example, the odds of winning each prize must be stated in the promotional material. Also, all prizes must be awarded, or an announcement must be made that some may not be awarded. The form of judging must also be explained. Despite these requirements, however, marketers seem to be returning to contests and sweepstakes in fairly large numbers since they provide so much excitement in the marketplace.

The number of sweepstakes conducted exceeds that of contests by about a 5-to-1 margin. The reason is that sweepstakes attract 5 to 10 times as many entries as do contests. Advertisers know that sweepstakes are a proven sales promotion tool to build interest.

The Difference Between Contests and Sweepstakes

The American Association of Advertising Agencies says, "A contest is an event that invites the consumer to apply skill to solve or complete a specified problem."[1] You're probably familiar with the kind of contest that asks you to finish a sentence on why you like a product, to add the final line to a jingle, to write a limerick, or to name a product or trade character. From the entries received, the winner is then selected for some sort of achievement. This is the crux of a contest, the requirement that skill be the basis for determining a winner.

In a contest, entrants may be required to provide a proof-of-purchase (a "consideration") to enter, or they may have to satisfy some other reasonable prerequisite in order to have their entry judged. Therefore, a contest usually has three basic ingredients: a prize or prizes, skill or knowledge as a basis for selecting a winner, and some form of consideration to enter.

The American Association of Advertising Agencies says, "A

---

[1]Sales Promotion Committee, American Association of Advertising Agencies, *Sales Promotion Techniques: A Basic Guidebook* (New York: American Association of Advertising Agencies, 1978), p. 30.

sweepstakes does not call for the application of skill on the part of the consumer. Winners are determined by a drawing from all entry forms. In other words, prizes are awarded on the basis of chance."[2] A sweepstakes requires only that a person submit his name, a number, or some other element in order to enter. The winner is usually selected from all entries received. No skill or knowledge is necessary. While a sponsor may suggest a proof-of-purchase or other form of entry eligibility, it cannot be required. If a consideration, such as a label or a proof-of-purchase, is required, the sweepstakes then becomes a lottery, which is illegal in all states. A lottery is defined as consisting of a prize, an element of chance, and a consideration. To avoid lottery laws, the sponsor of a sweepstakes may suggest that entrants submit a proof-of-purchase of the product, but it must clearly state that a reasonable facsimile will be accepted. In this way, the consideration requirement in the form of a purchase is avoided, and the lottery laws do not apply.

Types of Contests and Sweepstakes

Contests do not fall into neat, mutually exclusive, nonoverlapping categories. As we said, contests may be based on filling in the final sentence; naming the product; writing a limerick; estimating size, weight, or contents; and so on. The type is limited only by your imagination and what you want to accomplish.

Sweepstakes, however, can be usefully divided into types. According to Don Jagoda, of Don Jagoda Associates, the most popular types of sweepstakes are (1) the straight sweepstakes, in which the winning entry is drawn or selected from all those submitted; and (2) the matching sweepstakes, in which numbers or symbols are distributed, often through the media, and winners are determined by matching their number or symbol with one that has been preselected. The newest and most likely the fastest-growing matching sweepstakes uses a "rub-off" card. The entrant obtains a sweepstakes piece and simply rubs off the coating over a number or symbol. Then the usual matching procedure follows. While this type was originally developed by fast food operations, it is now being used by packaged goods advertisers. Cracker Jack, for example, in-packed 148 million "rub-off" game cards in boxes of their product in a recent promotion.

Another popular type of sweepstakes is called "programmed learning." The entrant is required to give back some information from the label, the package, or the advertisement. The respondent must read (and presumably "learn" from) the advertising message

---

[2]*Sales Promotion Techniques,* p. 36.

in order to submit the required information with the entry. Winners are chosen from among those who submit "correct" entries.

The Advantages

While contests and sweepstakes are definitely different in form and method, they offer the same advantages and disadvantages. They should be used primarily to supplement a regular advertising campaign or to build interest in a product or brand that has not been heavily promoted. By themselves, contests and sweepstakes are not very effective in developing trial users or attracting new ones.

The specific advantages of contests and sweepstakes are:

1. They can extend, build, or reinforce the image of the product. For example, by associating the product with an impressive prize structure, the marketer can make the product more impressive itself. Contests and sweepstakes can also be used to help establish or enhance the creative positioning of the product through the theme of the promotion.
2. Contests and sweepstakes often accomplish the difficult task of getting the advertising read. With the tremendous amount of competition for the consumer's time and attention, an exciting event such as a contest or sweepstakes can help break through advertising clutter and get readers involved in the advertising.
3. Contests and sweepstakes offer a method for getting retail on-the-floor display space, which other forms of sales promotion can't achieve. They can also help build retail traffic.
4. Contests and sweepstakes can give a product a needed "change of pace." For example, in a category in which emphasis has been on heavy couponing, the change in appeal provided by contests or sweepstakes can generate great attention.
5. Contests and sweepstakes can be used to direct the advertising and sales promotion effort against specific target markets. For example, the theme of the contest or sweepstakes and the prize structure can be developed and presented to appeal to specific demographic or psychographic segments of the population.
6. Contests and sweepstakes may sometimes be used to attempt to generate trial of a product, although they are not always effective in doing this. If the contest or the prizes are of sufficient interest, consumers may be lured into trial of the product just to participate in the event.
7. A contest or sweepstakes may also be used as a method of tying several brands or products into a single sales promotion program. This works particularly well for a marketer who has several brands or products in complementary categories.

Contests and sweepstakes aren't cure-alls. They have the following disadvantages as sales promotion techniques.

The Disadvantages

1. Usually, a contest or sweepstakes won't produce a big jump in sales or mass trial of the product. If this is the goal, another technique, such as sampling, will be much more effective. Contests and sweepstakes are better for building a long-term image than for eliciting an immediate response.

2. Widespread consumer involvement and product attention usually don't result from contests or sweepstakes. In fact, only about 20 percent of the population has ever sent in an entry for any type of contest or sweepstakes. In addition, approximately 75 to 90 percent of all sweepstakes entries are accompanied by a facsimile, not the proof-of-purchase that boosts sales. Thus, many people apparently participate in contests and sweepstakes without purchasing the product, and the expected sales gain for the marketer never occurs.

3. Another disadvantage is that this technique attracts many professional entrants whose only objective is to attempt to win the prizes, not to purchase or try the product.

4. Contests and sweepstakes usually require heavy media expenditure support to make them successful. Since the media message is usually devoted to the contest or sweepstakes, sometimes the same amount of money invested in more direct-action sales promotion techniques can be more effective in generating sales.

5. There is no accurate way to pretest a contest or sweepstakes program. As a result, major investments must be made strictly on judgment or on previous experience. In this respect, contests or sweepstakes are often risky ventures for the marketer.

6. Finally, the many rules and regulations at the federal, state, and local levels may make the development and implementation of contests and sweepstakes difficult for the marketer. Often, this type of promotion is prohibited in sales areas where it is needed most.

Some Guidelines

First, if you are planning any sort of major contest or sweepstakes promotion, we strongly recommend that you consult with a professional contest developer. While it is possible for you to develop and conduct a contest or sweepstakes on your own, the complexities of the rules and the maze of potential problems seem to call for the use of a professional organization, of which there are several. (See Appendix II for a list of organizations.) Whether you develop and conduct your own contest or sweepstakes promotion or use a professional organization, you'll want to consider the following suggestions.

Prizes

The prizes and prize structure of the contest or sweepstakes obviously have much to do with its success or failure. The usual prize structure is a pyramid, consisting of a major grand prize of great value, a series of smaller prizes of intermediate value, and a large number of prizes of small or token value. Often, the bottom prizes are samples of the product or are product-related in some way.

State-run lotteries are usually good indicators of the kinds of prizes that appeal to consumers. On that basis, it appears that prize structures with many intermediate-value prizes are not as popular as those with a very large grand prize. Supporting this view, Don Jagoda lists cash as the most appealing contest or sweepstakes prize, with at least $25,000 as the grand prize. Many consumers seem to be attracted to novel ways of distributing cash prizes, such as $1,000 a month for life. Second and third on Jagoda's list of popular grand prizes are vacation trips and automobiles. Jagoda also stresses that novel or unique prizes can be as attractive as the same or a greater value in cash.

Costs

Costs of developing and conducting a contest and sweepstake involve several things. For example, in developing a budget, one must include:

- The cost of the prize structure.
- The cost of the media used to promote the event.
- The cost of the entry blanks, point-of-purchase materials, and other support activities at both the consumer and trade levels.
- The cost of judging entries and notifying winners. Several organizations do this on a fee basis. In 1980, the cost of judging a straight sweepstakes with no requirement other than selecting a winner for a nationally distributed package good was estimated to be between $5,000 and $8,000. For a contest in which all entries must be evaluated, the cost of judging runs from $15,000 to $25,000, even though the number of contest entries is only one-tenth that of sweepstakes entries. The more requirements in the promotion, the greater the judging fee.[3]
- Incidental costs, such as legal fees and insurance.

---

[3]Personal correspondence with Don Jagoda, Don Jagoda Associates, New York, 1980.

Laws

Legal restrictions on contests and sweepstakes are quite complex. We strongly suggest that you seek legal counsel on the rules and regulations simply to avoid problems later. An excellent source of information is the *Federal Trade Commission Regulation-Rule for Games of Chance in the Food Retailing and Gasoline Industries.* This is available from the FTC, Washington, D.C. Because of the many state and local regulations on contests and sweepstakes, particularly in Wisconsin, Missouri, and Washington, you should also check the state statutes. In national promotions, state and local restrictions can be avoided by making the event void where prohibited by law. Again, however, qualified legal counsel should be used to prevent any problems from arising.

Rules

One of the major factors in assuring a successful contest or sweepstakes is to have clear, easy-to-understand rules. Although rules for every event will probably differ, the American Association of Advertising Agencies suggests that the following are applicable to all types of contests and sweepstakes:

- Include the closing date of the event.
- List the judging method and describe how ties will be broken.
- List the requirements for entry, such as: Who is eligible? What materials must be submitted?
- Outline the prize structure.
- Identify the judging organization. Be sure to state that its decision is final.
- Tell entrants that all entries become the property of the sponsoring organization.
- Make arrangements for announcing the winners. This is often done by providing a list to those who send their names and a return postage envelope.
- Explain how unclaimed prizes will be awarded.

The date of the contest or sweepstakes should be clearly stated, particularly the closing date. Two to three months is the usual length of most contests or sweepstakes. This usually gives sufficient time for proper marketing promotion and gives more entrants an opportunity to participate.[4]

According to Howard M. Turner, Jr., there are two basic reasons for setting up complete rules for a contest or sweepstakes: (1) to make sure that the entrant knows exactly what to do, and (2) to be

---

[4]*Sales Promotion Techniques*, pp. 37–38.

certain that the promotion fulfills all legal requirements. To achieve the first objective, Turner recommends the following models for giving directions to contest and sweepstakes entrants:

Contest. Fill in entry blank below with your name and address. Complete statement "I like product A . . . " in 25 words or less. Mail to Box XYZ. Mail with box top of product A.

Entry blank sweepstakes. Fill in entry blank below with your name and address. Mail to Box XYZ. (Describe proof-of-purchase or facsimile requirement.)

Lucky number sweepstakes. You may have already won. Compare the number of your card with winning number on product A display. If you have a winning number, fill in your name and address and mail this card by registered mail to Box XYZ.

Game sweepstakes. Obtain a game piece every time you visit our store. Affix game piece to corresponding spot on your game card. If you get five game pieces in a row, you are a winner. Take your winning card to our store for verification and awarding of specific prize.

To avoid legal difficulties, Turner suggests the following guidelines:

Qualification of entrants—eligible and ineligible. The sponsor of a sweepstakes or contest may limit the requirement for participation in any way he sees fit, as long as all within a classification are eligible. Thus, an automobile company can confine its promotion to all licensed drivers; a cigarette company can confine it to all entrants over 21 years of age. Rules should describe clearly all those who are eligible. In order to remove any suspicion of favoritism on the part of sponsors, members of the sponsoring company and its advertising or promotion agencies are almost invariably barred from eligibility.

Purchase requirements. Description of proof-of-purchase, or facsimile, necessary to accompany entry blank must be covered in detail (e.g., "Mail entry with bottom panel from carton of product A or with 3- × 5-inch sheet of paper on which you have printed words 'PRODUCT A' in plain block letters").

Frequency of entry. Notify consumer how often he can enter (e.g., "Only one entry per person" or "Enter as often as you like").

Information on expiration dates, date of drawing, and winners' notification dates. In sweepstakes or contests, the rules should specify the expiration date. Where entry blanks are involved, a cut-off date usually refers to a postmark date on the mailed entry. Date of drawing or completion of judging is usually also specified, as well as date by which winners will be notified.

Legal protection statement. In order to protect the sponsor from any possible legal complication, the rules usually state, "Void where prohibited by law." In cases of sweepstakes and games, "No purchase required" must be included in the rules, in bold type.[5]

There are, of course, many more details involved in developing and executing a contest or sweepstakes. Again, we strongly urge you to obtain expert assistance and legal counsel if you are planning a major contest or sweepstakes event.

In Figure 3-1 below, you'll find the rules for a contest conducted by Gillette Company for their "Soft & Dri" deodorant. This example provides some excellent guidelines on what you should include in your own contest.

FIGURE 3-1. Contest Rules

Source: William A. Robinson, *100 Best Sales Promotions* (Chicago: Crain Books, 1980), p. 96.

Some Examples

On the following pages, you'll find illustrations of some contests and sweepstakes that actually worked. They are presented in no particular order but were selected primarily to reveal the great variety of prize structures and themes, the many tie-in possibilities, and

---

[5]Howard M. Turner, Jr., *The People Motivators* (New York: McGraw-Hill, 1973), pp. 109–11.

the large amount of creativity that goes into developing a successful sales promotion event of this type.

Contests

Every contest requires some sort of skill or talent, which is the basis for judging the entries. A French's "Make-Your-Life-Delicious" Recipe Hunt required contestants to send in an original recipe using French's mustard. The "skill" element was in the development of the recipe. The grand prize was $2,500, and every entrant received a free cookbook—with recipes using French's products.

A White Horse Scotch whisky promotion required entrants to answer questions based on information on the back of the bottle (programmed-learning). The contest was tied directly to the product, encouraging entrants to visit the store, buy the product, and read the label. The promotion did its job. More than 266,000 consumers sent in entries. As a result, sales rose consistently during the contest.

Shasta beverages used a guessing contest: How many cans of Shasta will a Toyota Corrola hold? The contest gave local Shasta bottlers an opportunity to build in-store and mall displays through cooperation with Toyota dealers. The addition of Yamaha motorcycles and Murray bicycles extended the appeal of the contest to the prime market for soft drinks—teenagers and younger children. Adults, as well as teens, were interested in the grand prize, a Toyota Corrola. The inclusion of a cents-off coupon on the purchase of a six-pack of Shasta beverage enhanced the excitement of the contest.

The Saratoga cigarettes contest asked contestants to draw and submit a cartoon that used the theme of Saratoga's advertising at the time, "Wait 'til I finish my Saratoga." Again, skill was required, making the event a contest, not a lottery.

While these are just a few examples of the types of contests that have been developed, all illustrate the kinds of skills and talents contests require in the selection of a winner. They also show the many ways in which contests may be directly related to the product.

Sweepstakes

We've selected four sweepstakes to show how this technique may be used to help increase sales. Note that in most cases the event is tied directly to the product in some way. That helps reinforce any regular advertising or sales promotion supporting the brand.

The Monopoly "40th Birthday Sweepstakes"—"Win a Monopoly game filled with real money!"—was an excellent example of tying the sales promotion to the brand or product. It was a simple, direct, immediately appealing, and understandable idea, and it reinforced the product and the brand name. Most important, it worked. The entry rate, based on the circulation of the two women's magazines in which full-page ads were placed, was over 5 percent. Sales, too, increased 5 percent. Of course, there was no requirement for any consideration. Winners were selected by chance alone. And prizes totaled only $30,000.

FIGURE 3-2. Saratoga's Cartoon Contest
Source: William A. Robinson, *100 Best Sales Promotions of 1976/77* (Chicago: Crain Books, 1977), p. 70.

The Gold Medal "Golden Opportunity Sweepstakes" also illustrates how, by tying the prize structure to the product and the interest of the consumer, a sweepstakes can be developed at relatively low cost. Prizes included "a kitchenful of Frigidaire appliances," casserole sets, lasagna dishes, and Belgian waffle irons. Total budget was less than $55,000; yet the event drew nearly 1 million entries. That's the sort of response a good sweepstakes can generate, especially for a parity product suffering a seasonal slump.

The Benson & Hedges "100's Sweepstakes" is an example of an unusual prize structure that helped draw attention to the sweepstakes: 100 different prize categories, from 100 bunches of asparagus to 100 days' interest on $100,000 to a new car. Participants could enter any or all of the drawings separately. Again, no skill was required. Consumers were just asked to send in the entry blank and a proof-of-purchase (or reasonable facsimile). It was so successful, it has been used now for more than 10 years.

FIGURE 3-3. Benson & Hedges 100's Sweepstakes
Source: William A. Robinson, *100 Best Sales Promotions of 1975/76*
(Chicago: Crain Books, 1976), p. 51.

Finally, here's an example of a sweepstakes that should appeal to everyone. The Del Monte "$1,000 Coupon" was run in the top 50 ADIs (Areas of Dominant Influence) in the country, with 100 winners guaranteed in each ADI. The sweepstakes appealed to the trade, since the prize money had to be spent with them. Furthermore, the "$1,000 Coupon" was an excellent example of a total sales promotion package. Ads were run in Sunday supplements and *TV Guide*. Retailers named on winning entries received $50 bonus prizes. And all this was supplemented by attractive point-of-sale material. The results? Over 800,000 entries and sales of 9 percent over the quarterly goal.

The primary thing to remember about contests and sweepstakes is that they provide an excellent way to get additional readership for the advertising. That's very important when there is really nothing new to say about the product or if it is simply at parity with competition. We've found, too, that relating the contest or sweepstakes in some way to the product usually produces the best results. Don't simply offer something ordinary in a contest or sweepstakes, such

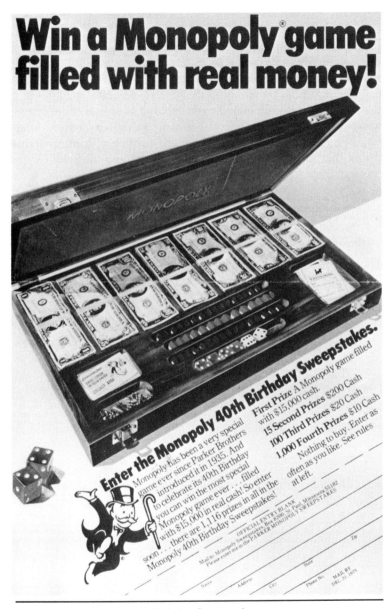

FIGURE 3-4. Monopoly's Birthday Sweepstakes
Source: Robinson, *100 Best Sales Promotions of 1975/76*, p. 38.

as a trip to Las Vegas or Acapulco. Build your contest around an idea that has some relationship to your product, your competitive claim, or the benefit your product offers the consumer. That's the kind of synergism that generates sales and profits.

Finally, the real success of a contest or sweepstakes is usually the theme or the prize structure that is developed. While these should be related to the product or the advertising being used, creative contest themes and exciting prizes can do much to build consumer interest and participation in an event. While the object of a contest or sweepstakes is to sell product—not to generate entries—dull, drab, unimaginative, look-alike contests and sweepstakes are often a waste of money. And, while cash usually generates the most interest, you can make your budget stretch further with merchandise prizes that have recognized values. Contests and sweepstakes are the real place for creativity in the sales promotion field.

Bonus Packs

One of the more widely used sales promotion tools in the consumer packaged goods field, particularly in food and over-the-counter drug categories, is the bonus pack. The technique works quite well in several product categories and many marketers use it on a regular basis. Unfortunately, little published information is available on bonus packs. This may be because each bonus pack is time- and product-specific, and the information may be applicable only to one product during one promotion period. But certain characteristics are common to all bonus packs.

The bonus pack normally consists of a special container, package, carton, or other holder in which the consumer is given more of the product for the same or perhaps even lower price than in the regular container. In effect, the extra product is a "bonus" for making the purchase—thus the name of the technique. You should not confuse a "bonus pack" with a reusable container. The incentive in the bonus pack is to obtain an additional amount of the product. The incentive for a reusable container is to obtain the container as premium and not necessarily the additional amount of the product. The idea of the bonus pack most likely sprang from the "baker's dozen," in which 13 units are given for the price of 12.

Since the bonus pack appeals primarily to the present or previous user of a product, it is most effective when used to solve product or product-related marketing problems. For example, if your objective is to increase the amount of the product purchased or used by the consumer or to increase the amount on hand, the bonus pack is a sound tactic. Also, competitive problems can often be solved by using a bonus pack. If, for example, your competitor plans to either introduce a competitive product or put a promotional push behind an existing product, a bonus pack can offset this promotion. Since

Introduction

the bonus pack puts more of your product in the hands of consumers, they are not as likely to respond to competitive offers.

The investment in a bonus pack includes the cost of the product itself, special packaging and special shipping containers (if the unit size has been changed), additional packaging and handling time at the plant and the warehouse, and (because bonus packs need more than shelf exposure to be successful) media advertising. Because bonus packs vary widely in size, shape, and value, however, and because each bonus pack is different in terms of the quantity packed or distributed, it is very difficult to give cost guidelines for this type of promotion. In most cases, the people involved in packaging and production are more qualified to determine these costs than is the sales promotion manager. We therefore urge you to get solid estimates for increased packaging costs and production costs (if any) of a bonus pack before proceeding too far with this type of sales promotion event.

Types   There are two standard types of bonus packs, with many variations. The first is a larger container with more product offered at the regular or reduced price. In essence, the package is simply made larger and extra product is included. This is illustrated by the Heinz Ketchup offer in Figure 4-1. The second type is a package made up of several units of the product banded together in some way so that an extra unit of the product is offered at a reduced price or even at no cost. In Figure 4-2, you will find an example of such an offer by Dial soap.

Notice that in the Heinz Ketchup offer the package is the regular size and shape of the familiar catsup jug, but is larger. In this way, Heinz was able to introduce a new size product by offering a bonus pack. The offer, which is clearly stated ("6 Ounces Free'), was supposed to appeal to both Heinz and other brand catsup users as well.

In the Dial soap example, four bath-size bars of soap were banded together with the offer of "Buy 3, get one free." This type of bonus pack is quite common in this product category. The obvious intention is to take consumers out of the market for a longer period of time. If they obtain four bars of soap at one time, there is less likelihood that they will respond to competitive offers while there is still plenty of product on hand.

Obviously, not all products can make use of the bonus pack sales promotion technique. For example, it would be quite difficult to offer two IBM computers for the price of one or to band two International-Harvester trucks together. Bonus packs are usually limited to products that are fairly low in cost, have simple packaging requirements, have high velocity (are used up quickly), and in which additional product is a desirable reward in the eyes of the consumer.

FIGURE 4-1. Bonus Pack: Larger Container

Source: Used by permission of H.J. Heinz Company.

FIGURE 4-2. Bonus Pack: Extra Unit
Source: Courtesy of Armour-Dial, Inc.© 1980 Armour-Dial, Inc.

Bonus packs are often used in an attempt to either reward or retain present customers. They can also be an effective way of getting attention at the point-of-purchase among parity products and are a sound way of presenting a price reduction to the consumer. With the bonus pack, the manufacturer is sure that the "extra" offer will reach the consumer rather than having the retailer absorb the reduced price or extra product as additional profit margin. When extra product is given as a bonus pack, the manufacturer's offer usually reaches the consumer at the shelf.

The Advantages

Besides giving a competitive edge by offering "more for the money," bonus packs provide several other advantages:

1. They are often effective in converting triers of a product into users. The savings is a reason to buy, and the extra product may encourage additional usage.
2. They make something happen on the retail shelf. Among parity products, a bonus pack stands out at the point-of-purchase and gives an extra incentive to buy. Often, bonus packs are effective in getting off-shelf displays in retail stores, particularly if the product is a major brand and is not easily shelved with the regular product.
3. Bonus packs can load customers with the product. In effect, if consumers take advantage of bonus packs and stock up, they are taken out of the market for a period of time. This is often

effective in counteracting competitive sales promotion programs.

4. They encourage repeat purchases. If the consumer is happy with the product, a bonus pack is an effective way to encourage another purchase.

5. Bonus packs can be used as the basis for an advertising event. When little else can be said about the product, a bonus pack says to the consumer, "Here is a way to save money." Thus, the consumer gets the impression of a larger size and value than other brands offer.

The Disadvantages

In addition to the fact that they are limited to certain products, there are several important disadvantages to bonus packs.

1. Bonus packs can be quite expensive. The cost of the additional product may be small, but the cost of the new package, the banding together of several packages, or other handling can be quite costly.

2. Usually, bonus packs do little or nothing to induce trial by the consumer. The feeling is, "If I don't buy or use Brand X, why would I want two instead of one?"

3. Bonus packs can be abused by the trade, particularly in those instances where units are banded together. Unscrupulous merchants can break the banding and sell the extra or bonus product at the regular price. Thus, the proposed offer never even reaches the consumer.

4. Bonus packs really do nothing for the brand image of the product. This sales promotion technique is a form of price reduction and is usually of little help in building up the quality image of the product or contributing to long-term growth.

5. Bonus packs usually require special handling. This is often a problem for both the manfacturer and the retailer. Because bonus packs often don't fit on shelves, they must be relocated to other areas. Many retailers won't accept bonus packs for this reason.

Some Examples

Below are illustrations of some of the various methods of offering bonus packs. Note the variations and how each is "flagged " or "specialed" to call attention to the offer at the point-of-purchase.

Figure 4-3 is an example of a free or added product offer. In this case, Maxim coffee offered 9 ounces of coffee for the price of 8, or one free ounce, when the product was purchased. Notice how the offer is clearly stated on the product package. In a category such as coffee, in which brands may be substitutable, this type of promotion at the shelf can help build sales.

FIGURE 4-3. Bonus Pack: Maxim
Source: Reproduced courtesy of General Foods Corp., owner of the
registered trademark Maxim.

Figure 4-4 is another example of an added unit at no cost. In this
case, Bic shavers offered one free razor with the purchase of three.
Here, the attempt was to build sales for a new product and this one
worked.

Almost everyone with a packaged product can take advantage of
the bonus pack idea. For example, Figure 4-5 shows one of the
world's leading marketers using the technique. A six-pack of 16-
ounce Coca-Cola cans was offered at the price of the 12-ounce cans,

FIGURE 4-4. Bonus Pack: Bic
Source: Photo courtesy of BIC PEN CORPORATION.

promising "Twenty-four extra ounces of Coke free." That's an incentive most consumers would find hard to pass up in the retail store. And the promotion usually builds extra sales.

To show there is really nothing new in the world, only variations of old ideas, Figure 4-6 illustrates the bonus pack idea implemented by Keebler for its "Elfwich" brand cookies. As we said at the beginning of this chapter, one of the first bonus packs was probably

FIGURE 4-5. Bonus Pack: Coca-Cola
Source: Courtesy The Coca-Cola Company.

FIGURE 4-6. Bonus Pack: Keebler
Source: Courtesy Keebler Cookie Co.

the "baker's dozen." Keebler makes that idea work with a real "baker's dozen" by including a free dozen cookies in its bonus pack. That's a good promotional idea.

Bonus packs can and do work. It's knowing how to implement them that really makes them pay off in sales.

Stamp and Continuity Plans

Although they rise and fall in popularity, trading stamps and continuity programs are still very important and effective sales promotion techniques. These programs may appear in varying types of formats, but all have the common goal of building repeat purchases for a product or repeat visits to a retail store. The most common forms of this sales promotion program involve the consumer in either (1) collecting stamps, labels, or proofs-of-purchase, which are to be redeemed for prizes; or (2) making multiple purchases of the same product or visiting the same store several times to collect a complete set of items, such as dishes, cookware, or towels. Usually, continuity offers are made over fairly long periods of time, since the consumer often has to make several purchases or visits either to collect the premiums or to purchase enough of the product to satisfy the requirements for the prize or premium.

The major difference between stamp and continuity programs and other forms of sales promotion is the time lag between the product purchase or store visit and the receipt of the reward or gift. With most forms of sales promotion, the consumer reward is immediate, as in a price reduction through a coupon, a reusable container, or a bonus pack. With a continuity program, however, the consumer must purchase the product and save the stamps, coupons, or proofs-of-purchase over a period of time in order to receive the reward.

Stamp and continuity programs are most effective in solving certain types of sales promotion problems. They seem to work best in situations where the objective is either to build repeat purchases or to protect present purchasers from competitive activities. Normally, once consumers enter a continuity program by saving stamps, labels, or proofs-of-purchase, they are reluctant to switch to another

61

brand. Thus, this technique is quite effective in solving product or product-related sales problems and is also effective in offsetting competitive promotions.

Types

We separate continuity programs into four major types.

Trading Stamps

Trading stamps are issued with each dollar's purchase at retail stores. They are saved by consumers and then redeemed for prizes from a catalog. A prime example of this type of program is the Sperry & Hutchinson "S&H Green Stamps" plan, as illustrated in Figure 5-1.

While trading stamps are major sales promotion tools, we have purposely not included descriptive material on them in this section simply because they tend to be a form of long-term retail merchandising. They are not usually considered practical in package-goods sales promotions.

Manufacturer-Originated Continuity Programs

Continuity programs using stamps, coupons, or other forms of proof-of-purchase by manufacturers are not as widely employed as they have been in the past. Several plans still exist, however. A prime example is the Betty Crocker coupon, which appears on General Mills products. In this type of continuity program, the consumer is encouraged to purchase products bearing seals or stamps on a regular basis in order to obtain various premiums free or at reduced prices. A Betty Crocker coupon is illustrated in Figure 5-2.

Another example of a continuity program of this type is the Raleigh cigarette promotion, which has been conducted for many years. In this program, coupons are included in packs of cigarettes, and additional coupons are given for the purchase of cartons. The consumer saves the coupons and redeems them for prizes available through a prize book.

Pack Continuity Programs

In- or on-packed premiums are another method of conducting a continuity program. In this approach, the prize or premium is either attached to the package or in-packed with the product. For example, Breeze detergent has been including facecloths and towels in its packages for several years. By purchasing various sizes of the product, the consumer can build a complete set. In programs such as the Breeze detergent promotion, the continuity program is an integral part of the marketing plan for the product and is continued month after month.

FIGURE 5-1. Trading Stamps
Source: Courtesy of the Sperry & Hutchinson Co.

Another form of in- or on-pack continuity program is the limited duration plan. For example, a prize or premium is offered when the consumer sends in three labels or proofs-of-purchase to the marketer. These short-term promotions differ from the continuity programs because consumers must collect the necessary labels or proofs and submit them in a relatively short period of time.

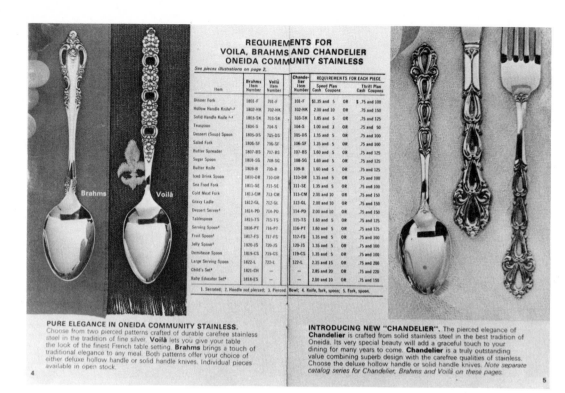

FIGURE 5-2. Continuity Coupons

Source: Courtesy of General Mills, Inc.

The Nestlé "Free Guinness Book of World Records" (see Figure 5-3) requires proof-of-purchase in the form of two inner seals from packages of Nescafe Instant Coffee. While this promotion technique could also be considered a free premium, we mention it here to show how various promotional plans are often either combined or blended.

These limited-time continuity programs are much more popular with package-goods marketers than are the continuing plans. They give the company an opportunity to build interest in topical items and then change the offer to reach new or different customers and prospects. There is increasing emphasis on this type of promotion as marketers attempt to build brand loyalty.

Store Continuity Programs

The fourth type of continuity program is that employed by retail stores or outlets to build continued patronage. Chief examples of this type of program are those conducted by food stores and supermarkets. They may consist of premium offers, such as that illus-

FIGURE 5-3. Limited-Time Continuity Plan
Source: William A. Robinson, *100 Best Sales Promotions of 1977/78*
(Chicago: Crain Books, 1979), p. 110.

trated in Figure 5-4 for the Jewel Food Stores' stoneware promotion. Each week, a different piece of stoneware was offered at a reduced price. Consumers could return to the store each week and, by purchasing the various pieces, build a complete set of stoneware. In addition, various additional serving pieces were also offered at reduced prices, so that a complete service could be obtained. This is typical of the product promotions carried on by food stores and other types of retailers across the country.

Last call for cereal bowls! Don't miss out on savings at Jewel! Cereal Bowl 49¢ each

If you need more cereal bowls to finish your stoneware place settings, this is the last week to purchase them at Jewel. Pick up the bowls you need for just 49' each with each $5 purchase — they won't be offered again.

And you still have time to add accessory pieces that will serve you in style from morning 'til night. There's a covered butter dish to serve with morning toast, soup bowls for the kids' lunch, even coffee mugs for your last cup of the day.

Come to Jewel this week — our stoneware savings are going out with a bang!

Complement your stoneware with versatile serving pieces!

12" Decorated Chop Plate	$6.99	Gravy Boat with Stand	$5.99
Covered Sugar	4.99	Covered Casserole	9.99
Creamer	4.99	Coffee/Tea Pot	9.99
9" Round Vegetable Bowl	5.99	12" Oval Platter	5.99
Salt & Pepper Shakers	4.99	10" Oval Baker	5.99
Covered Butter Dish	5.99	2-pc. Soup Bowl	4.99
		2-pc. Mug Set	4.99

Weekly schedule

THURS., APRIL 24 WED., APRIL 30	Cereal Bowl

Jewel

Come to Jewel for the quality, you'll come back for the price!

Sunshine Flowers

Highland Flowers

Prairie Flowers

FIGURE 5-4. Store Continuity Program
Source: Courtesy Jewel Food Stores.

In addition, food stores and other retailers conduct various types of games that offer prizes for winning tickets or game pieces acquired in store visits. While this has traditionally been a retail promotion, it is no longer so limited. In spring, 1980, United Airlines offered the first major continuity game program in the air travel field. In what it called the "Take-Off" game, United offered 10,000 free trips during the month of April. This was quickly followed by American Airlines' "Baseball" game and TWA's "Win the World" promotion, both of which offered similar prizes. All three were designed to build continuity in airline usage. (See Figure 5-5.)

FIGURE 5-5. Continuity Game Program

Source: Eugene Mahany, "Promo Techniques Spread Wings," *Advertising Age*, April 28, 1980, p. 60.

On the following pages, we will discuss stamp plans and continuity programs together, since the objectives, advantages, and disadvantages are much the same. We will also review food, retail store, and manufacturer's continuity programs briefly. The basic objective of all continuity programs is to encourage more frequent, multiple, or repeat purchases. It is simply an attempt to gain consumer loyalty through a means other than product quality or satisfaction or to set the product apart from competition in a parity product category.

The Advantages

When a consumer participates in a stamp or continuity program, one of the chief aims of the program has been achieved, to gain participation, which in turn should build brand loyalty. That is the single most important reason to use this type of sales promotion technique. In addition, marketers have found stamp and continuity programs can:

1. Create differences between parity products. Given a choice between brands with little visible distinction, a continuity program can be a differentiating feature, particularly at the point-of-purchase, to help influence the actual sale.
2. Be a fairly low-cost substitute for a higher-budget, brand-image-building advertising campaign. The continuity program and the premiums can be used as something the advertiser can talk about in his media advertising to call attention to the product.
3. Take consumers out of the market by loading them with the product. They can also be used to extend the use or the seasonality of the product. Once customers start saving, they usually want to continue to do so in order to obtain the prize or gift, regardless of the season or the traditional time the product has been used.
4. Be a low-cost add-on promotion as part of a larger, more lasting advertising and promotional program. The continuity prize or gift can also be used to reinforce other brand advertising.

The Disadvantages

The major disadvantage of this type of sales promotion technique is that substantial amounts of money must often be tied up in inventory in order to fulfill the continuity merchandise offers. Once a marketer commits himself to a continuity program, there are few ways to stop the plan until it has run its course. Other disadvantages are:

1. Usually, continuity must be run a long time. For example, if a premium such as a radio is offered for 50 stamps and the average purchase gives the consumer two stamps per week, the program must run a minimum of 25 weeks to avoid disappointing many savers.
2. Continuity programs don't appeal to a great many consumers. Many people today are not willing to wait or to save for the premiums or prizes. They want immediate gratification.

3. Continuity programs seldom get off-shelf displays and have little appeal to the retailer. As a result, sales to the trade are seldom increased through this type of sales promotion program.

4. Continuity programs do not necessarily work for all types of products. For example, they are often not effective for infrequently purchased products. Price, however, doesn't seem to be a problem; industrial marketers have used continuity programs on many relatively expensive products.

Some Guidelines

Because of the major investment of both time and money in developing any type of stamp or continuity program, we strongly urge you to contact a consultant or organization that specializes in these programs. Usually, such programs are quite complex, require a great deal of handling, and can be quite expensive if not properly planned. Here are some general areas that should be given particular attention:

1. The objectives of the continuity program. Will the program run for a short period of time and offer a number of coupons or proofs-of-purchase for obtaining one specific item, or will it be an ongoing program in which several prizes or gifts are available over time? Each has a different set of objectives, costs, and sales promotion implementations.

2. The type of proof-of-purchase or coupon required. Some products and packages lend themselves to easily providing a proof-of-purchase or label. Others, however, aren't so simple. Getting a proof-of-purchase from a plastic or metal container is sometimes nearly impossible.

3. The number and cost of premiums. This is a key element in the success of any continuity program. If the prize structure is limited to one item, has it been pretested for consumer acceptance? A program offering a prize or gift with little or no appeal is usually worse than no program at all. What will be the cost of the premium? Can you afford it, based on the selling price of the product? Finally, what about the availability of the prizes? Nothing upsets consumers more than to save for a gift and then find it's not available.

4. The structure of the program. Will you accept only proofs-of-purchase or can cash be substituted? If the premium is to be packed in the product, in what size packages will it be available?

5. The length of time of the offer. It must be long enough so that the average consumer will be able to save sufficient stamps or coupons to obtain the gift.

6. Handling the fulfillment of the offer. Will the prize or gift be distributed through stores, through the mail, or how? And who is to accept the orders, check them, and then distribute the premiums?

All of the above questions and more must be answered in the process of setting up a stamp or continuity program. That is why we suggest that one of the organizations listed in Appendix II be consulted. They are experienced in the area and can give tremendous help.

Some Examples

Sales promotion continuity programs vary widely. On the following pages we have illustrated a few of the most successful ones in the past few years. While these may or may not be applicable to your brand, based on the market situation and your needs, they do give a broad view of various types of continuity programs and explain how each was conducted.

Campbell Soup's "Labels for Education"

This continuity program had very wide appeal, and is considered a "classic." Schools wishing to participate in "Labels for Education" submitted forms indicating the choice of school equipment they wanted (i.e., gymnasium, audio-visual, sports, etc.), along with the quantity of labels necessary to redeem the items. It was a program that served the needs of the public and no doubt built both sales and goodwill for Campbell.

Post Cereal's "Box Tops For Fun 'N Fitness"

PTA's, school boards, education associations, and individual educators were all interested in saving Post cereal box tops to receive free sports equipment. Prizes ranged from bats to trampolines. More than 30,000 schools participated. This too was a promotion that built not only sales but good will as well. (See Figure 5-6.)

Post Cereal's "GAF View-Master and Super Heroes Picture Packet"

To build sales for the Post line of ready-to-eat cereals, General Foods combined five brands in a single continuity program. The offer was a $5 value GAF View-Master, plus a picture packet of the "Super Heroes," free with nine proof-of-purchase seals from any of the participating cereals. If consumers couldn't wait, they could send in two proof-of-purchase seals and $3. Either way, this promotion was probably a winner for Post. And to make sure it was, Post distributed 30¢-off coupons on the purchase of any two Post cereals.

FIGURE 5-6. Continuity Program: Post Cereal

Source: William A. Robinson, *100 Best Sales Promotions of 1976/77* (Chicago: Crain Books, 1977), p. 27.

Scotties Tissues Variable Continuity Program

Scott Paper took the continuity idea and offered a "variable" program, based on the number of "Seals of Quality" saved from Scotties Tissues. Consumers decided how and when they wanted to cash in on this offer for free boxes of Scotties. By saving two seals, purchasers were entitled to one free box. They could get two free boxes with four seals and three free boxes with six seals. It was a novel twist to the old idea of building sales through a continuity program.

Food or Retail Store Continuity Programs

Food or retail store continuity programs are quite different from those conducted by the manufacturer. Some examples are:

1. "Game" sweepstakes conducted by stores or chains, which offer several levels of prizes. These programs are usually purchased from suppliers who provide all the necessary materials, promotional plans, and prizes.
2. Set-building premium offers, such as dishes, encyclopedias, silverware, and so on. In most instances, a certain piece is offered each week for a period of time. By shopping the store each week and purchasing featured products or buying a certain amount, the consumer can build and eventually complete a set.
3. Tape programs in which premiums or products are offered free or at a discount for saving a certain total value of cash register tapes. Again, these are usually syndicated programs that the retailer simply buys and implements in his store or stores.

We've found that retail store promotions provide some exciting exceptions to the disadvantages listed above for product continuity programs. For example, 35 percent of all food store shoppers have participated in a food store continuity program. Even more important, more than 12 percent of the shoppers have actually switched stores to participate in some kind of continuity promotion at the retail level. Those are impressive figures when compared to the usual effect continuity programs have for individual products.

To conduct a successful retail or food store continuity program, we've found the following points are important:

- You must advertise the offer. That means regularly, not just once to kick off the promotion. Every week is best.
- You must give the offer prime display space in the store.
- You must have the support of the in-store personnel to help maintain interest in the program.
- You must offer quality merchandise, particularly with a premium program, to build the store's "value" image.
- You should plan the program for no more than 10–15 weeks. After that time, the interest of the consumer and the store personnel starts to fade rather quickly.

One thing that should be considered when developing a retail continuity program is how much emphasis the program should be given in overall promotion plans. If you overemphasize the plan or the continuity program, you may find that you're advertising and promoting premiums instead of the store's image or features. That's a real hazard. The line between enough and too much emphasis on the continuity program is quite fine.

Price-Offs

A price-off means a reduction in the price of the product. It can also be translated into a reduction in margin for the marketer. It is favored by some manufacturers and feared by others. The most common reason for a price-off is the need to match or beat competitors' prices. But price-offs can be used as more than a defensive weapon. They can also be used offensively to generate additional sales, which may translate into increased market shares and/or long-term profits.

Introduction

While price-off promotions may be used effectively in many marketing situations, they seem best suited to overcoming competitive situations. By competitive situations, we mean those cases in which either the competition has made changes in its marketing activities that have created problems for your brand or there is a likelihood that such changes will be made. Such situations may include:

- Product pricing problems, in which competition has either increased or decreased the price of the product at the wholesale, retail, or consumer level.
- Introduction of a new competitive product or a line extension.
- A competitive reformulation, repackaging, or addition of new ingredients to existing products.
- A disruptive competitive activity, either through pressure on present dealers or by an invasion of the market by an outside brand.
- A new, revised, or increased amount of competitive advertising in the marketplace at any level.
- A new, revised, or increased amount of competitive sales promotion at any level.
- An increased or improved competitive trade deal at the wholesale or retail level.

While these are certainly not all the problems that competition can create for a brand, they are the most common. Certainly, they are the ones that can be effectively combated by a price-off promotion.

Most manufacturers use price-off promotions to hold present customers or to counter competitive moves. Such promotions work well in gaining consumer attention at the point-of-sale among parity brands and serve as a method of increasing impulse purchasing. Often, price-offs can be used to encourage consumers to trade up to a more expensive brand. For example, if the price-off offer reduces the price to the approximate level of less expensive brands, then the consumer may be encouraged to try the product.

Most price-off merchandise seems to be purchased by younger, higher-income, better-educated, urban, married couples. It is also attractive to large families with children.

Many manufacturers fear price-offs because they believe that the price of the product should never have to be reduced. They seem to think that the product should always be sold at the originally established price. However, in today's active market, with roller-coaster prices, that isn't very feasible, at least for most products. While it is true that too many price-offs can damage the brand's image and reputation, not enough can create serious sales problems. The secret is getting just the right mix.

The Advantages

Whether they are used offensively or defensively, price-off promotions have many advantages.

1. They can be used to hold present customers. The price-off is an immediate cash reward or saving to consumers for buying. Thus, it is a good method of holding them or keeping them buying the brand, since they have already found it to be satisfactory.
2. Price-offs can head off competition by loading or taking customers out of the market. Price-offs encourage consumers to load up or buy more than the normal amount of the product. They stockpile the product since most "price-offs" are for a limited period of time. When they do this, they really have no need for additional products. Thus, when a competitive promotion occurs, they will have a sufficient supply and will not be in the market.
3. Price-offs can be used to establish purchase patterns after initial trial. If you have used another form of sales promotion, such as sampling or couponing to gain initial trial, a price-off event will often help convert the trier into a regular

user. This approach seems to be particularly effective with low-cost, frequently purchased package goods.

4. Price-offs are a sure method of getting a reduced price offer through the trade channels to the consumer. Since the offer is made directly on the product, a pass-through of the savings to the consumer is almost assured. There are few ways for the wholesalers or retailers to absorb the planned consumer saving in the distribution channel.

5. Price-offs create on-shelf attention for the brand. Since competitive products are displayed next to or near your brands, a well-flagged or colorfully promoted price-off on the package can create attention on the shelf. It can set your brand apart from competition.

6. Price-offs, particularly when combined with a trade allowance, can be used to generate an off-shelf display for the brand. The combination of a price-off and trade deal makes a strong promotion offer to the retailer. Usually, retailers will extend this promotion into the store in the form of a dump or an end-aisle display.

7. Price-offs are extremely flexible. The manufacturer has total control over the number of units being promoted and the areas in which the offer will be made. Price-offs can be moved in and out of the marketplace as needed, although there are some legal restrictions. They are an excellent "fire-fighter" tool in competitive situations.

8. Price-off promotions can be easily controlled by the manufacturer. As many price-off packs as needed can be labeled and shipped to retailers. In this way, the marketer knows in advance exactly what the promotion will cost.

9. Price-offs can be used to create the impression of a larger size or value to the consumer. In competitive situations at the shelf level, a price-off pack can help offset competitive maneuvers such as in-packs, coupons, and the like.

10. Price-offs can be used to boost the sales of a particular size, flavor, or brand in the line. For example, if sales of the small size of the product need a boost, a price-off can be added only to that size to encourage additional purchases.

11. Price-off promotions protect the trade profit. Since the manufacturer is taking the price reduction, the trade margin can be maintained at the traditional level. This is a particularly appealing feature to most retailers.

12. The price-off technique gives the sales force extra ammunition to use in selling to the trade. Since the price-off is usually limited in quantity, it can be used as a device to load the trade against competition.

13. Finally, the price-off is an excellent tool to help accelerate an upward sales trend. If the product is moving well, the price-off sales promotion device seems to be one of the best methods of increasing that gain.

The Disadvantages

With all the advantages of price-off promotions listed above, it might seem they are the best tool available for any situation. Unfortunately, there are several disadvantages too.

1. A price-off can give the brand a sales bump, but it usually can't reverse a downward sales trend. In other words, like most sales promotion techniques, a price-off can be used to generate an immediate sales increase but can't be used to make up for major product problems, declining sales in the category, or other factors that may have initially caused the downward sales trend.
2. While the price-off may give a market share increase, the increase is usually only temporary. The price-off is an incentive to purchase now. When the incentive is removed, the product usually falls back to its previous sales levels.
3. Price-offs don't produce loyal new customers. The incentive is to save. When the saving is removed, many customers return to their previous brand or to another brand that offers some other incentive to buy. For example, some studies have shown that price-conscious consumers return to private label purchases when the price-off on a major brand is no longer available.
4. Repeated use of the price-off promotion often degrades the perceived value of the product. As a result, sales increases from continuous price-off promotions become increasingly smaller. Apparently, when used too often, the price-off becomes simply a part of the brand as an accepted fact. As consumers become accustomed to it, it becomes less and less effective. It also gives the impression that the brand is always "on sale." When it isn't, sales usually don't occur.
5. The smaller the brand share, the larger the price-off required. For this reason, price-offs are not usually a good tool for brands with a small market share. Part of the reason may be that the perceived value of the brand is not known. Thus a larger reduction of the price may be needed to persuade the consumer to purchase the product.
6. A price-off is not usually a good method of gaining trial. We've found that on-packs, couponing, and sampling are much more effective in getting trial of a product than is a price-off sales promotion program.

7. From both the manufacturer and trade view, price-offs require considerable special handling. Since a price-off pack must be a separate manufacturing run, production costs of materials and processing often increase. The same situation occurs in handling the price-off cartons in the warehouse. Both manufacturer and retailers incur extra costs in keeping them separated from regular priced merchandise.

8. In addition to creating handling problems for the retailer, price-offs may also create inventory problems. The retailer obviously wants to take advantage of the price-off promotion, but he may already have regular-price inventory. This may cause inventory imbalance.

9. Price-off promotions may not be widely accepted by the trade. The handling, inventory, and stocking problems often discourage use. The trade also has less interest in a price-off package simply because it is available to all other retailers. Therefore, it offers no specific competitive advantage. Estimates show that only about 50 to 60 percent of all food and drug retailers will accept a price-off promotion for use in their stores.

Unfortunately, because price-offs vary so greatly in terms of timing, costs, and production, it is not possible to get very specific about how to use them. There are, however, some general guidelines.

Some Guidelines

Planning

Price-offs require a great deal of coordination and cooperation throughout the entire manufacturing organization. Since the development of the price-off pack is essentially a manufacturing process (i.e., special labels must be affixed or special cartons used in the production run), the production department, the shipping and storage people, the sales force, the wholesaler, and the retailer must all be coordinated so that the promotion is carried out smoothly. A price-off is usually not something that can be done overnight.

The method of display of the price-off offer on the package is critical to its success. While there is always concern with the attractiveness of the label or feature area, the clarity of the offer and its visibility on the shelf outweigh most aesthetic considerations. If the customer can't see the price-off, it simply won't work. A bold burst (a jagged-edge price spot) or flag (a box printed over the regular label) is best, with the amount clearly stated. Don't hide the offer.

Generally, a direct price-off will produce faster direct-sales action than any other form of offer. The more complicated the price-off, the lower the interest in the promotion by the consumer.

Costs

Two cost factors should be considered when evaluating a price-off promotion. The first is the cost of the price reduction. This is a fairly straightforward calculation. Simply multiply the number of units on which the price-off is to be used by the amount of the reduction. For example, if the price is to be reduced 10¢ per unit on 100,000 units, the total cost of the reduction would be $10,000. An additional cost that is not quite so easy to calculate is that of the special labels and cartons. Since art work, plates, and special printing are involved, this cost will vary for almost every offer, depending on what is to be done. The production people are the ones most qualified to determine these costs.

Pricing

Price-offs must usually be a minimum of 15 to 20 percent off the regular retail price to have much effect with the consumer. As we said before, brands with smaller market shares must usually offer larger reductions than the brand leaders to achieve similar sales increases. Price-offs are also usually more effective for a new brand than for an established brand. New brands can also offer a smaller price reduction than established brands to maximize sale. Usually, the larger the price reduction, the faster the sell-through to the consumer. As you might expect, larger reductions attract more new triers at the retail level.

Usually, smaller quantities offered at greater price reductions will provide larger share increases than offers in which the reduction is smaller but the quantity of goods available is larger. In addition, price-off deals of 6-7 percent usually have little effect on the product's competitive position no matter what the brand's sales are or the amount of merchandise offered. Lesser reductions only attract the brand's regular users.[1]

Some retailers don't like price-off promotions by manufacturers because they may reduce the profit on the product. For example, most retailers calculate their profit based on what they pay for the product. Thus, if they buy a product for 50¢ and take a 20% margin, the retail price of the product to the consumer or the shelf-price would be 60¢. When a manufacturer reduces the price of the product by a set amount through a price-off on the shelf-price, he thus reduces the retailer's margin too, unless some adjustment is made.

The trade profit on any price-off promotion must be protected.

---

[1]Charles Frederick, Jr., "What Ogilvy & Mather Has Learned About Sales Promotion," a speech given to the Association of National Advertisers, September, 1973.

That is, you must usually give the trade a margin equal to or greater than the one being passed through to the consumer through the price-off. For example, if the trade normally receives a 20 percent margin on a product that retails at 50¢ (10¢ per unit) and the price-off to the consumer is 10¢, then the retailer's margin declines to 8¢ per unit on each sale unless an adjustment is made. In this case, it might be necessary to increase the retailer's margin to 25 percent on the price-off packs to make sure the traditional profit is still received on each unit sold. Note that if this is done, the extra discount to the trade on the price-off must be included as a cost of the promotion.

Estimating Supplies

While the supply of price-off units may be estimated on several different bases, it is typically figured as a certain number of weeks of estimated product movement. In other words, the number of price-off units to be offered is determined on the basis of previous or estimated week's sales. Let's assume that sales of Product Alpha have been 100 per week. The manufacturer estimates that sales will increase by 20 percent with the promotion. Thus, if the promotion is planned to run 5 weeks, 600 units will be produced (100 units per week plus a 20 percent increase, or 120 units per week × 5 weeks). Usually a 4- to 8-week supply of the price-off merchandise is planned for the average promotion. If the promotion is not being offered in all areas, the promotion amount can be determined by using previous sales or shipments to the specific areas involved.

FTC Regulations

The Federal Trade Commission regulations covering a price-off sales promotion program are quite specific. Generally, the FTC requires that:

1. Price-offs may be utilized only by brands with an established retail price.
2. No more than 50 percent of the total volume of a brand may be generated through price-packs or price-offs in any 12-month period.
3. Only three price-pack (or price-off) promotions per year are allowed on any one brand size. A 30-day period must also be allowed between each of the price-pack offers on the brand.
4. A price-pack (or price-off) must be accompanied by display material that gives the following information clearly:

Brand name	Brand X
Regular price	78¢
Cash savings	12¢
New price	66¢

A retailer who uses this technique must indicate the regular price, the price reduction, and the new price.[2]

You should consult your legal counsel for other legal factors that may affect price-offs or price-packs for your brand or category. Also, check to make sure that you are in compliance with all current regulations.

Bursts and Flags

When designing a "burst" or a "flag," remember it's more important to get the price reduction across so shoppers can see it than it is to have the price look esthetically pleasing. The only real require-

FIGURE 6-1. Price-Off: On the Label

Source: Reproduced with the permission of Hunt-Wesson Foods, Inc.

[2]Sales Promotion Committee, American Association of Advertising Agencies, *Sales Promotion Techniques: A Basic Guidebook* (New York: American Association of Advertising Agencies, 1978), pp. 31–32.

FIGURE 6-2. Price-Off: On Flexible Packaging

Source: William A. Robinson, "Five More 'Best Promotions' Share
the Facts and Shed Light on Marketing Success," *Advertising
Age*, April 3, 1978, p. 52.

ment is that the price reduction not be so large that the general
identification of the label is impaired. Shoppers often select products by color and label design, so don't overwhelm the label with
the "price reduction"—just make sure it's visible at a glance.

Some Examples

Because price-offs vary so widely, it is impossible to give examples
of all the various ways in which this promotion may be presented.
Shown below, however, are examples of the more typical methods.

On the Label

The standard label for the product can be revised with a burst, flag, or other device to announce the price-off. In Figure 6-1, Hunt's offers a price-pack with 4¢ off on tomato sauce.

On Flexible Packaging

The use of flexible packaging often creates problems for price-offs, but Bic used a price-off on its packaging quite effectively, as Figure 6-2 illustrates.

Banded Packs

An alternative to the cents-off on the label or package is banding together several units of the product and offering a price-off on the combination. This is quite common in the bar soap, chewing gum, and candy categories. (See Figure 6-3.)

One-cent Sale

A fourth choice is to offer two or more packages or cartons of the product at a reduced price. For example, "Buy one, get one free"; "Three for the price of two"; or the ever-popular "Buy one, get another for 1¢." Figure 6-4 illustrates how Walgreens handled this type of promotion. Note that in addition to offering the second item for only 1¢, Walgreens took the promotion a step further by offering a "Match or Mix" addition. The customer could purchase a one-cent sale item at the everyday price and get a different Walgreens product for 1¢ more. The customer was charged for the higher-priced of the two items, plus 1¢. The "Match or Mix" offer was limited to items advertised in the section. This is just another way to build interest and excitement in a promotional event.

As more and more emphasis is placed on self-service and marketers rely more and more on consumers to make their purchasing decisions at the store and at the shelf, it is likely that price-offs will become more and more important in marketing and sales promotion.

FIGURE 6-3. Price-Off: Banded Items

Source: Courtesy of Armour-Dial, Inc.

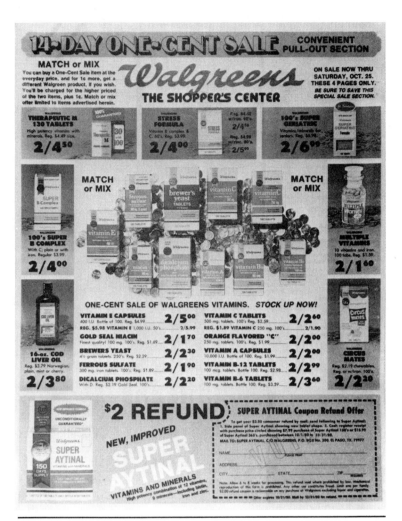

FIGURE 6-4. Price-Off: One-Cent Sale
Source: Courtesy of Walgreens.

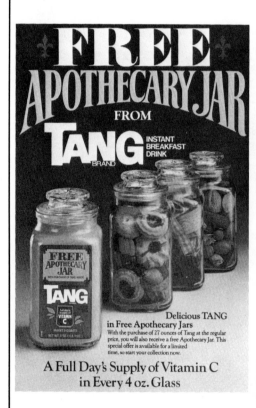

In-Packs, On-Packs, Near-Packs, and Reusable Containers

Introduction

Just as the names imply, special pack promotions consist of free offers, premiums, or packages that are given with the purchase of a product. We distinguish them from the more traditional premiums because they are not mailed in for future redemption but are offered as an immediate reward to the consumer. The primary purpose of these special packs is to call attention to the product on the shelf and to provide a point of difference, particularly in a parity product category. The various techniques known as in-packs, on-packs, near-packs, and reusable containers are named primarily for the method in which the premiums are either attached to or otherwise available with the product. We will cover this in more detail below.

While in-packs, on-packs, and near-packs can be used to solve many types of marketing problems, they are particularly effective in competitive situations. For example, a premium can be used to overcome a competitive price advantage or to offset a competitive coupon offer. In addition, if the premium has an obvious value, the consumer may even be willing to pay a slightly higher total price for the product and premium than for the product alone. When all products are at parity, the offer of a premium with a purchase is an effective way to obtain off-shelf or special area displays for the product.

In-packs, on-packs, near-packs, and reusable containers are particularly effective in encouraging trial of a product. The reasoning is that if the consumer buys the product to get the premium and is satisfied with the product, he or she will continue to use it on a regular basis. Thus, if the premium provides the reason for the trial purchase, it will have been well worth the cost.

87

Types Although on-packs, in-packs, near-packs, and reusable containers can be used for similar purposes and for solving similar problems, there are some important differences among them. They not only look different; they are also typically used in different product categories.

In-Packs

The in-pack premium is placed inside the package—thus the name. Although the premium is usually small and fairly low-priced it can range in size and value up to towels, sheets, and dishes packed in detergent boxes. The in-pack is widely used in the health and beauty aids categories. Probably the most famous in-pack premiums are those in ready-to-eat cereals and Cracker Jack candied popcorn (Figure 7-1).

On-Packs

An on-pack is a premium attached to the product or product package in some way but not placed inside the package. For example, it might be banded to the product, attached with a rubber band, or blister packed. On-packs may also be items such as coupons, cutouts, and the like, which are printed on the carton or box. Sometimes, the product and the on-pack premium are related: shaving creams with razors, canned cat foods with plastic can covers, and recipe booklets with spices.

Near-Packs

The near-pack is a premium offered with the purchase of the product at the point-of-sale. Usually, because the item is too large to on-pack, it is put in a separate display near the product. When the consumer purchases the product, he or she is entitled to take one of the near-pack premiums. The distinguishing feature of a near-pack when compared to a regular premium is that the consumer is immediately rewarded with the premium rather than going through some ordering process. For example, Lever Brothers, working with the Marvel Comic Group, developed a special near-pack Spiderman comic book to be given with Aim Toothpaste. The comic book itself focused on proper dental care as a story line. And Lever got total mileage out of the promotion by featuring a "Birthday Sweepstakes" on the back of the comic book. In some instances, a slight charge may be made for the near-pack premium, particularly if it is a fairly expensive item. In such cases, it is often called a salable or price-plus pack.

Reusable Containers

The reusable container is also a form of premium that accompanies the purchase of a product. The distinguishing characteristic is that

FIGURE 7-1. In-Pack Premium
Source: Cracker Jack® is the trademark of Borden, Inc., for candied popcorn and peanuts.

the product is packed in a container that can be used after the product has been consumed. The most common premium of this type is the venerable "jelly glass" that graces most of the homes in the U.S. Once the product is used up, the container continues to be used. Another example of the reusable container is Libby's tomato juice packed in a decanter. Obviously, the attraction to the consumer was not only the prospect of enjoying Libby's tomato juice but also the acquisition of a container that could be put to other uses in the home at no extra charge.

Most consumer products marketers have used some sort of in-pack, on-pack, near-pack, or reusable container at one time or another. For example, cosmetics manufacturers have used free tote bags with the purchase of a certain amount of their product; cigarette manufacturers have offered on-carton premiums, such as cigarette lighters; fast food chains have offered free, collectible soft drink glasses; cereal manufacturers have used in-pack toys, and games; and children's foods have taken advantage of near-packs of toys, games, and puzzles.

One of the important values of in-packs, on-packs, near-packs, and reusable containers is their ability to influence impulse sales. If the consumer is ready to purchase some brand or is at the shelf, the premium may very well be the extra incentive that sways the choice in the direction of the promoted brand. In-, on-, and near-packs can also be effective in getting consumers to trade up to a larger or more expensive brand in the line. In some instances, if the premium is exciting enough, it can even be the extra incentive for getting in-store displays.

The Advantages

Because they vary so widely in usage and opportunity, we will discuss each of the different approaches separately. All, however, have certain advantages in common, which we have already discussed, such as influencing impulse sales, getting trade-up sales and off-shelf displays, and giving the appearance of extra value.

In-Packs and On-Packs

The major advantages of these promotional tools are:

1. They can differentiate the product at the point-of-sale, which is important if the competition is at parity.
2. Often, in- or on-packs can extend the advertising to the point-of-sale. If the offer is also made in media advertising, the two can work synergistically. The consumer sees the media advertising and then is reminded of it at the store.
3. In- or on-pack premiums can be developed to appeal to specific segments of the market. If the idea is to appeal to children, a certain type of premium may be used. If the target group is adults, then another premium can be used, and so on.
4. If the premium is related to the product, it can increase usage. For example, if a recipe book is packed with a sack of flour, it may suggest additional ideas to the consumer and increase usage of the product. Similarly, a coffee mug might increase the consumption of coffee; or soup bowls, the consumption of the soup brand.
5. The cost of in-pack or on-pack promotions is known in advance. Because the marketer knows exactly how many of the

special premium packs have been manufactured and shipped, there is much better control of the costs of this sales promotion tactic. The number may be increased or decreased to conform to the budget requirements.

6. In-pack or on-pack premiums will generally create a larger number of new triers than price-off merchandise. In fact, if properly selected, the appeal of a premium is usually greater than a reduced price. This may be because in-packs and on-packs offer the consumer a greater value than the actual cost expressed as a "price-off" on the product. That is, the premium is often worth much more than the amount of a normal price reduction.

Near-Packs

The major advantages of near-packs are:

1. They are a sure way to get a display. If the retailer accepts the offer, he is committed to display the near-pack adjacent to the product.
2. Larger premiums can be used. Because there is virtually no limitation on what may be offered (except that it must be practical), larger and more impressive premiums can be given with near-packs.
3. Near-packs are extremely flexible. Since they are not directly connected to the product, they can be added, taken away, or moved at will.
4. Near-pack premiums can increase the use of the product. This is particularly true for products requiring a large or unwieldy premium intended to extend use of the product, such as leaf bags with a rake or lighter fluid with charcoal.

Reusable Containers

The advantages of reusable containers are:

1. Because they replace the regular packaging, the extra cost can be added to the value of the premium. Thus, a better offer can be made.
2. If the container is quite attractive, or serviceable, the price of the entire product can be increased. This may help offset the cost of the premium. For example, if a handsome coffee carafe were used as a container, the coffee normally selling at $3.00 might be increased to $3.50 to cover part of the cost of the carafe.
3. A properly selected container can increase the use of the product. For example, margarine might be packed in a series of

reusable plastic bowls. To obtain the complete set, the consumer would have to continue purchasing the brand or to use more while the offer was available.

4. If appealing enough, the reusable container can be used in an off-shelf display at retail. This works particularly well if combined with some other sales promotion device.

The Disadvantages

While these sales promotion devices are usually very effective, they also have some disadvantages.

In-Packs and On-Packs

The potential extra cost of attaching the premium to the product is the major disadvantage. In addition, we believe the following are also important.

1. Although a premium is always expected to have a positive effect, it may not. In- and on-pack premiums should be pretested to assure success. If the premium doesn't provide an incentive to the customer, it obviously isn't worth the cost, no matter what the price. Testing costs money. Not testing, however, may be more expensive in the long-run. The question is how much can you afford to spend in testing to assure success?

2. Poor in-pack or on-pack premiums can actually hurt sales. If the consumer is ready to buy and sees an on-pack or in-pack premium that has no appeal, the sale may actually be lost on the spot. A previous bad experience with the premium can also reduce sales. A poor premium can prevent even regular purchasers from buying.

3. The size or shape of the premium attached to a product as an on-pack can prevent proper shelving.

4. If the premium is extremely attractive and not well packaged, theft or pilferage—by consumers or store personnel—can be a problem.

5. The use of in-packs and on-packs can also create inventory problems for the manufacturer and the retailer. Some retailers refuse to accept products with these types of premiums simply because they are not willing to inventory them in addition to the regular product.

6. Overuse of in-pack or on-pack premiums can cheapen the image of the product. If this type of device is used too often, the consumer might begin to look at the product simply as a premium carrier and not as an attractive usable product.

Near-Packs

While they can be quite effective, near-packs have limitations.

1. Near-packs are often hard for retailers to handle because they require additional space for a separate display. Near-packs may also create a problem at the checkout, since sales clerks must understand and follow through on the offer and make sure that only purchasers receive the premium.
2. The retailer may not promote or distribute the near-pack. For example, the premium may not be made available, may not be properly promoted in the store, or may be put back as stock and sold as a separate item. The sales promotion manager has no control over the near-pack after it leaves his hands. It may be a failure simply because of lack of retailer cooperation.
3. With a near-pack, there is always the problem of theft or incorrect redemption. Theft may come from the consumer or store employees. Incorrect redemption may result from poor attention at the checkout or lack of store control.
4. Often, retailers will not accept a near-pack premium that competes with a product they stock and sell for a profit. For example, if a wagon is used as a near-pack premium with a purchase of a lawnmower in hardware stores, dealers may not want to handle the premium simply because they sell wagons too. Dealers don't want to give away premiums they could be selling at a profit.

Reusable Containers

Reusable containers have the following limitations.

1. If they are not a standard size, they may be hard to shelve or store. In these cases, retailers may refuse to stock the item.
2. Unattractive or unwanted reusable containers can actually hurt sales. Consumers see the premium as part of the product. If they don't want the container, they may not want the product either.
3. If the container is also being sold in the store, the retailer may resist stocking. "Why give away something that can be sold?" is usually the retailer's philosophy.
4. Inventory can be a problem for both the manufacturer and the retailer. In addition, reusable containers may require packing in unusual or nonstandard cartons or containers. This may create handling problems at all levels.

With these advantages and disadvantages of in-packs, on-packs, near-packs, and reusable containers, you should have a good view of whether or not this sales promotion technique can work for you.

The primary decision is still whether or not the use of an in-pack, on-pack, near-pack, or reusable container will help generate additional sales.

Some Guidelines

As is the case with some other sales promotion devices, it is difficult to make more than a few generalizations about this particular technique. Uses, types, products, and needs vary so widely that much more specificity isn't really possible. We've found, however, that the following concerns are most important to someone considering the use of in-packs, on-packs, near-packs, and reusable containers.

Premium Value

The amount that a manufacturer can invest in a premium or a reusable container is usually constrained by the selling price of the product and the margins available for promotion. Interestingly, the cost of near-pack premiums and reusable containers has been increasing, while manufacturers have been attempting to reduce the cost of in-pack and on-pack premiums. This attempt has been only partially successful, however, since these premiums must always be specially wrapped. In addition, they must be packaged in such a way that they do not create a health hazard for children who might eat them or otherwise injure themselves with them. Manufacturers have become quite concerned over the type of premium that can be used, and this has limited the type of product that can be packed. In spite of these problems, we suggest the following cost guidelines:

1. In-packs. Premiums should range in cost from ¾¢ to 15¢ each. The low end is used with high velocity, relatively low-price products, such as ready-to-eat cereals. Higher-cost premiums can be used with more expensive products.
2. On-packs. Premiums usually range in cost from 10¢ to 20¢. Some may be higher but they are usually keyed to the retail price of the carrier product.
3. Near-packs. Costs can vary widely but they are usually based on what can be spent on the product promotion. Near-packs with a perceived value of less than $1 are usually not very successful.
4. Reusable containers. Depending on the price of the product, costs can range from 10¢ to several dollars. Much depends on the amount available for promotion and on how much of the cost can be passed along to the consumer.

Premium Selection

A vital part of premium selection is based on pretesting in some form. Some general rules apply to all premiums, no matter how they are used. The premium must:

1. Be easy to understand. The premium must require no explanation. What it is and how much value it provides must be
   absolutely clear. There is no time at the point-of-purchase to
   sell the premium.
2. Appeal as an impulse item. Since the premium is designed to
   gain immediate attention, it should be instantly appealing and
   make the consumer want to have it.
3. Be a brand name, if possible. An unknown premium is not
   nearly as attractive as one whose name and value are known.
4. Have apparent quality and durability. Premiums that look
   cheap or poor in quality can sometimes do more harm than
   good.
5. If possible, have a direct relationship to the product carrying
   it. While more than 80 percent of all in-pack, on-pack, or
   near-pack premiums are not directly related, we've found the
   ones that are do much better—for example, a creamer with
   coffee or a bowl with dog food.
6. Relate to the promotion theme. It does little good to have a
   promotion theme with one message and a premium featuring
   another message. The two should be tied together.

Finally, the premium to be used should be as distinctive as possible. Common, low-priced premiums that are available in any store
usually have little appeal. In addition, retailers don't want to promote products they could be selling. If the item is somewhat ordinary, such as a cup, bowl, or tote bag, it is best to have it identified
with the product name, logotype, or emblem. This makes it distinctive and generates greater appeal for even common items.

Rules and Restrictions

Very stringent regulations have been established by the Food and
Drug Administration on the type, form, and size of articles that can
be in-packed in food products. This is to protect consumers (and
manufacturers as well) from accidental eating or choking, especially
by children. In addition, there are restrictions on how the premium
may be packaged, the type of printing ink that can be used, and so
on. If you are considering an in-pack, be sure to learn about and
follow all the regulations on in-packing premiums in your product
category.

For on-packs, federal regulations are not as stringent. The major
concern is to provide a method of attaching the premiums that will
withstand shipping and possible attempts to break them up at retail. Some of the more common methods of attaching the premiums
are: banding, blister-packs, shrink-packs, neck ponchos, rubber
bands, and, of course, printing coupons or other materials on the
cartons or packages.

Costs

While most of the cost of this sort of premium promotion seems quite obvious, there are some that might be overlooked:

1. The cost of the premium itself.
2. The cost of printing, inserting, banding, or any other method of affixing the premium onto or putting it into the package. In the case of near-packs the cost of shipping should be included. The same is true for reusable containers if additional packaging is required.
3. The cost of any additional handling, either in the plant, in transit, or at the warehouse.
4. The cost of premium redemption, if one is included, particularly for coupons or bouncebacks.
5. The cost of inventory, advance purchases, or stock that must be held to provide additional near-packs or reusable containers.
6. The cost of point-of-purchase materials, such as posters, signs, coupons, or other in-store materials to promote the device.
7. The cost of media advertising to support the promotion.

There may well be other charges, such as licensing or legal fees for specific products. This is particularly true when the premium is a copyrighted item or is being purchased from an outside supplier.

Timing

In-packs, on-packs, near-packs, and reusable containers require considerable lead time to reach the market. The premium must be selected, the carton or package designed and printed, the premiums inserted or attached, and the product shipped to the retailer and then stacked on the shelves. Therefore, these devices are not ordinarily used as "fire fighters" in a competitive situation. We estimate that approximately 18 to 24 weeks should be allowed to develop and implement a good in-pack, on-pack, or near-pack promotion. For a reusable container, allow approximately 4 months.

Expert Help

Premiums such as those we have been describing can be quite expensive. A simple in-pack premium may involve thousands of dollars, particularly if it is used on a widely distributed brand that sells quickly. If you don't have personal experience with this type of sales promotion device, we suggest you contact one of the many premium experts available. You'll find some sources listed in Appendix II.

While it would be impossible to describe all the various types of offers or premiums that can be or have been used as in-packs, on-packs, near-packs, and reusable containers, some of the more common and successful ones are presented below. This will give you an idea of the range of promotional opportunities available.

Some Examples

In-Packs

Some of the most experienced and successful in-pack premium users are ready-to-eat cereal manufacturers. For example, Figure 7-2 shows one of the many Cap'n Crunch in-pack offers. Note how well it ties in with the image of the product.

As the Clinic shampoo promotion shows (Figure 7-3), almost anything can serve as an in-pack premium. In this case, Clinic is clear blue, so the gold charm in-packed in the bottle is easy to see and an obvious incentive to purchase. The premium truly reinforces the sales message in this instance, since the consumer can see the premium. This sales promotion idea came from Colombia, South America.

On-Packs

To be effective, an on-pack premium should add to or extend the use of the product carrying it. Figure 7-4 shows how Gillette on-packed a Good News razor with its shaving cream to do just that. One reinforces the other.

For several years Good Seasons® brand salad dressing mix has used a mixing cruet as an on-pack premium. The cruet not only extends the use of the product; it actually makes the product easier to use. In a recent promotion, Good Seasons® brand salad dressing mix also added a 20¢-off coupon to make the offer even stronger. That's the type of synergism that gives simple sales promotion ideas real selling power.

Near-Packs

More and more marketers are coming up with outstanding ways to use near-packs in nearly every product category. For example, Lever Brothers offered a free baseball-card pack with the purchase of Mrs. Butterworth pancake syrup. The offer was made simply and clearly: "Take one pack with your purchase of Mrs. Butterworth's." Nestlé gave away a 5-pound bag of sugar with the purchase of two 12-ounce packages of chocolate morsels. By buying a Toyota, consumers received one of seven items valued at $100 or

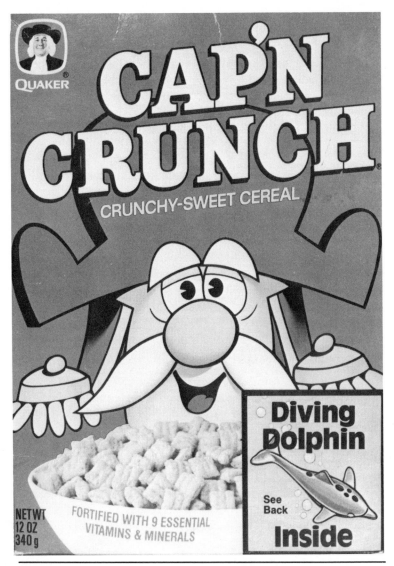

FIGURE 7-2. In-Pack Premium: Cap'n Crunch Cereal
Source: Courtesy of The Quaker Oats Company.

more, including binoculars, watches, and cameras. "Toyota buys you a gift," the copy read. "But what a gift!"

Reusable Containers

A reusable container that extends the use of the product is always a plus. A reusable container that will be used over and over with the

FIGURE 7-3. In-Pack Premium: Clinic⁺ Shampoo

Source: William A. Robinson, *100 Best Sales Promotions* (Chicago: Crain Books, 1980), p. 133.

product is even better. The wine carafe from Paul Masson gave a definite reason for selecting the product (Figure 7-5). Our guess is that there are many of those carafes still in use, most likely with Paul Masson wines.

Tang brand instant breakfast drink used a free apothecary jar to

FIGURE 7-4. On-Pack Premium: Gillette Shaving Cream
Source: Courtesy of The Gillette Company.

FIGURE 7-5. Reusable Container: Paul Masson Wine

Source: Courtesy of Paul Masson Wine.

promote sales. With the purchase of a 27-ounce package of Tang, the consumer, for a limited time, got an apothecary jar at no additional cost. As you can see, General Foods illustrated some of the uses of the jar to build interest (Figure 7-6). Tied to the free container was a 25¢ coupon that no doubt helped clinch the sale.

There are literally thousands of items that have been or could be used as in-packs, on-packs, near-packs, and reusable containers for many types of products. A good way to get new ideas is simply to keep in contact with premium suppliers. In addition, stay current by following the trade press and the latest teenage interests. Often, they can guide you to successful new ideas.

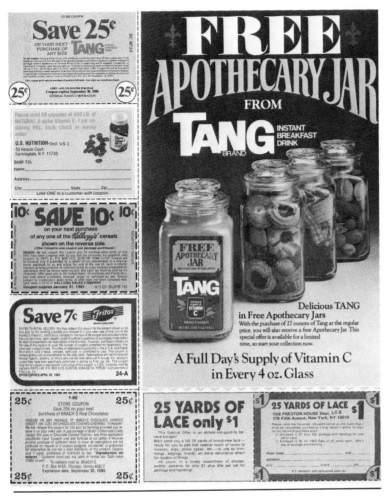

FIGURE 7-6. Reusable Container: Tang Breakfast Drink
Source: Reproduced courtesy of General Foods Corp.

Free-in-the-Mail Premiums

Although it is similar to the in-pack, on-pack, and near-pack premium and is closely associated with various forms of continuity premiums, we consider the free-in-the-mail premium to be a unique sales promotion tactic. Its sales objectives are usually different from those of the other promotional events. From the consumer view, the major difference between a pack promotion and a free-in-the-mail premium is that the latter is not an immediate reward, as are the in-pack, on-pack, and near-pack. Instead, the consumer must send in the required proofs-of-purchase or other evidence and then wait for the premium to be delivered through the mail. The free-in-the-mail premium differs from continuity premiums in that the offer is usually of short duration, while continuity premiums may continue for months and even years.

The most common free-in-the-mail offer consists of a premium that the consumer obtains by some evidence of purchase or use of the product. The evidence can be labels, UPC codes, price circles, trademarks, or any other items that may appear on or with the product and can be used to indicate that the product has been purchased. By simply mailing in these proofs-of-purchase, the consumer receives the premium through the mail.

Free-in-the-mail promotions seem to work best in competitive situations, although they can be used to meet many other sales promotion objectives. They are most effective when products are at parity and there is little product difference apparent to the consumer. Thus, the incentive to purchase the product and to continue purchasing it is transferred to the premium from the product. The free-in-the-mail premium approach assumes that there will be consumer satisfaction with the product. If there is a product defect or the product is not at parity with competition, then the expected

Introduction

103

repeat purchases will obviously not occur and the promotion will be a failure.

Free-in-the-mail premiums are estimated to account for only about 2 percent of all promotional offers. While this seems like a low figure, the technique is nevertheless very important and appears to be gaining favor with marketers.

To be effective, most free-in-the-mail offers require media advertising to support them, in addition to on-pack attention in the form of call-outs or bursts. Point-of-purchase displays can also be an effective method of promoting the offer, particularly to the impulse shopper. Media are used because the goal of a free-in-the-mail offer is usually twofold: (1) to get new users and (2) to keep present customers buying and loyal to the brand.

The Advantages

Among the strengths of free-in-the-mail premium offers are:

1. They reward present customers. Because present customers are already buying, it is easy for them to obtain the premium. This helps build brand loyalty and may even increase purchase patterns and usage.
2. They help guard against brand switching. If consumers are saving labels or proofs for a free-in-the-mail premium, they are not as likely to switch to a competitive brand until they have obtained the premium.
3. The offer of a free premium in media advertising usually increases readership of the advertising considerably. If the premium is attractive, people will want to learn more about the offer and, as a result, will read the advertising more thoroughly.
4. When a free-in-the-mail premium is combined with a cents-off coupon, response is increased by as much as 10 percent. It's an efficient and effective way to get and build product trial.
5. They can be used to build multiple purchases. Since most offers require several proofs-of-purchase, the consumer will often stock up on the product to get the premium more quickly rather than purchase at the normal rate.
6. More expensive premiums can be used. Since free-in-the-mail offers have low redemption rates, more expensive premiums can be used with the same total outlay for the promotion. In many cases, consumers start to save proofs-of-purchase for the premium but never get around to sending them in. This is called "slippage." It means that the sales promotion device generated extra sales, but no actual redemption resulted.

7. Free-in-the-mail premium promotions are fairly easy to set up and control. Once the offer is made, the only chore is to return the premiums as the orders come in.

8. They can be used to trade the consumer up to a larger size or more expensive brand. If the customer has been using the small size and a free-in-the-mail offer is made on the larger size, the customer may purchase the larger size simply to obtain the premium.

9. Free-in-the-mail premiums can be used as "dealer loaders" or to obtain off-shelf displays. A "dealer loader" is a premium that is used as part of a display in the store. When the promotion event is over, the store manager is allowed to keep the premium. In this way, the premium can be used to obtain an order and a display from the retailer. He has been "loaded" with the product. Often, free-in-the-mail premiums are given to the dealer for display or as a reward for stocking the product.

The free-in-the-mail premium is not without its disadvantages.

The Disadvantages

1. Sales increases are not usually measurable. Redemption of the premium seldom runs over one percent of the gross media circulation. It is not an extremely strong business-building technique.

2. With the requirement of multiple proofs-of-purchase, new users will not generally be attracted to the premium offer as much as present users will be.

3. The premium is not immediately available. With the increasing problems of mail service and delivery, many consumers are not willing to wait several weeks to receive the premium through the mail.

4. In most cases, media advertising is required to make the offer successful. Since the intent is to bring new purchasers to the brand, it is necessary to promote the promotion to make it effective. That money might be better spent in another manner.

5. A free-in-the-mail premium is not a strong impulse-purchase item. Since multiple proofs are usually required, the appeal to purchase now is not as strong as with other sales promotion techniques.

6. Free-in-the-mail offers are extremely hard to test prior to use. Since the requirement is for multiple purchases to obtain the product, few people can accurately tell in advance how they will actually react to the offer.

Some Guidelines

Because free-in-the-mail premiums are so difficult to test, most knowledge about them is purely empirical. We have the following ideas and suggestions for most types of free-in-the-mail premiums, regardless of the type of offer.

Premium Selection

Generally, unusual premiums pull best. Some of the better ideas have been a forehead fever thermometer offered by Kleenex and Anacin, a free designer bracelet by Quencher™ cosmetics, a "Keep Fit America" exercise booklet from Geritol, the "Perfect Coffee Book" from Maxwell House, a 30-foot Chinese kite from Chun King, and a racing patch from CAM2 motor oil.

Ideally, free-in-the-mail premiums should have two important features: (1) they should reinforce the brand name or the brand image of the product being promoted, and (2) they should help increase the use of the product making the offer. Unfortunately, there is not enough creativity in this area of sales promotion. Many marketers return to "tried and true" premiums year after year. That's unfortunate since we've found that unique or novel premiums do quite well. Often, the best free-in-the-mail premiums are brand-name merchandise or premiums that have a known value to the consumer.

Costs

As we said earlier, fairly expensive premiums can be offered by marketers since they are betting that the redemption of the premium will be low. Thus, since redemption of free-in-the-mail premiums is usually only 1 to 2 percent of gross media exposures, a valuable premium can be offered with the assumption that the cost will not be high.

In addition to the cost of the premium, though, there are other costs with this type of sales promotion device:

1. Postage to return the premium. Often this is charged to the consumer as a handling fee. If it is not, it is a cost to the advertiser.
2. Packing and handling the premium. This includes the redemption facility to take care of the orders and the material necessary to ship the premium to the consumer.
3. Any promotional material to be used in the store or returned with the premium, such as a "bounce-back" offer.

Experience shows that it is usually best to pay a fulfillment house to handle the orders and shipping of free-in-the-mail premiums.

Unless you have the necessary people and equipment to handle fulfillment properly, it's best to let experienced people handle it. Some fulfillment houses are listed in Appendix II.

Promotional Methods

Traditionally, two methods have been used to promote a free-in-the-mail premium: media advertising and point-of-purchase material. Usually, more emphasis is given to media activities, since the idea is to bring new triers to the brand. The most common media used as promotional vehicles are newspapers and magazines.

The product package is also used as a means of promoting the offer. Since this type of sales promotion device has limited impulse-purchase appeal, on-shelf is a relatively weak method of promoting the offer.

The Offer and the Return Coupon

Unfortunately, one of the major problems with free-in-the-mail premiums is that sometimes the marketer makes it difficult for the consumer to understand the offer and even more difficult to obtain the premium. We strongly suggest that the offer be made as clearly and as simply as possible. Forget the "arty look." When practical, show an example of the proof-of-purchase required and tell how to remove it, where it is located, etc. Make it as easy as possible for the consumer to meet the requirements you have set for redemption.

One of the biggest problems is the coupon order blank. Be sure all the information you need to fill the order is on it. Make the spaces large enough for the person to write his or her name. Don't forget the zip code and other pertinent data. Figure 8-1 illustrates what we consider to be a clearly stated offer and an easy-to-understand coupon.

A Purchase Alternative

In some instances, consumers are willing to pay a certain amount of the cost of the premium to obtain it more rapidly. While this kind of offer is still technically free-in-the-mail, it requires fewer proofs-of-purchase but some cash. This method seems to be increasingly popular on many products.

An example of this alternative is shown in Figure 8-3 for a "Morris the Cat" T-shirt. The consumer could receive the shirt free with 30 9-Lives cat food labels, send in $2.75 with 10 labels, or pay $5 and mail in no labels. Thus, the marketer is able to offer a free premium but give the consumer a choice of waiting or not. We are confident that this type of approach will continue to grow in the future.

A little help in your kitchen –
free from Kellogg's.

Free ⓕⓞⓛⓔⓨ Nylon Kitchen Utensils for 3
Cracklin' Bran proof-of-purchase seals.

These convenient, high-quality Foley
Kitchen Utensils are yours free, just for enjoying the great taste and high-fiber goodness
of Kellogg's Cracklin' Bran. They're made of
lightweight, dishwasher-safe nylon that
won't scratch nonstick cookware surfaces.
Send 3 proof-of-purchase seals and receive
your free set of Foley Kitchen Utensils. Enjoy
cooking with Kellogg's.

*Foley is a registered trademark of Foley Manufacturing Co.

MAIL TO: FOLEY KITCHEN UTENSILS OFFER
P.O. Box 9125, St. Paul, MN 55191

Please send me ____ set(s) of Foley Nylon Kitchen Utensils. For each set ordered, I enclose 3 proof-of-purchase
seals from the side panels of Kellogg's Cracklin' Bran
cereal packages.

NAME _____

ADDRESS _____

CITY _____

STATE _____ ZIP _____

FIGURE 8-1. Free-in-the-Mail Premium Order Blank
Source: Courtesy of Kellogg Company.

Some Examples

Because there seem to be as many premiums offered through the mail as there are advertisers, it's impossible to cover all the potential premium ideas here. Since we have already discussed the most effective premiums, we will now illustrate some of the major objectives that free-in-the-mail premiums can achieve.

Expand Product Use

As we have said, the best premium is the one that either adds to, extends, or encourages additional use of the product. The offer in Figure 8-2 for a Prestone antifreeze coolant tester was a sure bet to expand the use of the product. The assumption was that if the consumer checks the antifreeze in the car regularly he is probably going to buy more.

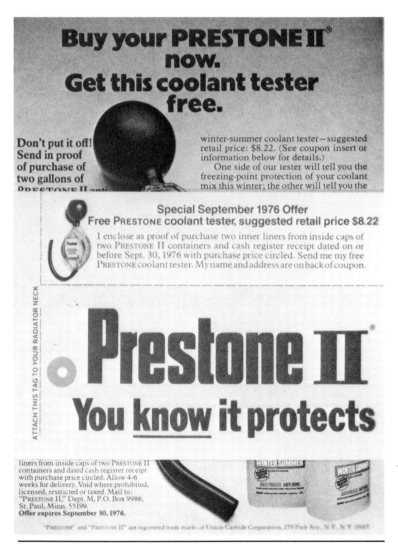

FIGURE 8-2. Free-in-the-Mail Premium: Prestone Antifreeze

Source: William A. Robinson, *100 Best Sales Promotions of 1976/77* (Chicago: Crain Books, 1977), p. 107.

Extend the Advertising Campaign

What better way to promote a product than to have thousands of people wearing or showing your advertising theme or advertising slogan as a piece of clothing? That has been done successfully over and over by advertisers with free-in-the-mail premiums. The "Morris the Cat" T-shirt is an excellent example of this type of offer. (See Figure 8-3.)

FIGURE 8-3. Free-in-the-Mail Premium: 9-Lives Cat Food
Source: Robinson, *100 Best Sales Promotions of 1976/77*, p. 105.

Tie-in with the Product

When it isn't possible to extend the use of the product or expand usage, successful free-in-the-mail premiums can often be developed that are product related. One example is the free coffee offer made by General Electric with its Coffeemaker: "Buy any GE Immersible Coffeemaker now and get 3 cans of MAX-PAX 'ELECTRA-PERK' Blend ground coffee filter rings free!" In return for a proof-of-purchase, the consumer got coupons exchangeable for the premi-

FIGURE 8-4. Free-in-the-Mail Premium: First Federal of Chicago
Source: Robinson, *100 Best Sales Promotions of 1976/77*, p. 100.

um. Land O' Lakes offered a cookbook calendar for 6 proofs-of-purchase or $1 and one proof-of-purchase. Of course, all of the 40 recipes in the cookbook called for butter among the ingredients. A somewhat more tenuously product-related offer was made by Fruit of the Loom. The purchaser of one of the many company products could receive 10 free strawberry plants (worth $2.70) merely by mailing in the order blank and 25¢ for postage and handling. Also available was a 50 percent savings on a variety of fruit trees.

Tie-in with an Event

When it isn't possible to tie the premium to the product or the advertising, it can sometimes be related to some current event of great interest. That's what First Federal of Chicago did with its "Free Rose and House Plant Offer" (Figure 8-4). This promotion was used every spring for a number of years when consumer interest was high in plants, growing, and gardening.

We consider these samples of the various types of free-in-the-mail offers to be sound ones. To repeat, if at all possible, free-in-the-mail promotions should extend use of the product or reinforce the advertising theme. This is the best purpose for this type of sales promotion technique.

Self-Liquidating
Premiums

Often referred to as "the old reliable" sales promotion tool, self-liquidating premiums have changed dramatically in the past few years. The idea is still the same. The consumer sends in enough money to cover the cost of the premium, postage, handling, and taxes, if any, so that the only expense for the marketer is the cost of the promotional effort. Recently, however, there have been several exciting changes. For example, not too long ago it was thought that the best self-liquidating premiums were those priced under $1. Now, however, you'll find some self-liquidating premiums ranging in price from $35 to $50 and more. It was also believed that premiums of this type should appeal to everyone or at least have a very broad base. Now, however, we have seen promotions successfully directed at very small, select audiences which have helped build sales for the brand. Things are changing in the self-liquidating premium field.

The self-liquidating premium may be the most widely used, and perhaps misused, of all premium forms. Traditionally, marketers have used it because it was low in cost, required practically no advance planning, and was easy to set up and handle. In some instances, it was used because "we couldn't think of anything else." Indeed, the self-liquidating premium has often been overused by marketers who were simply seeking something to talk about in their sales plans. If there is a primary fault of the self-liquidating premium, it is simply that it is used with little or no planned objective by some marketers because it is so easy and convenient to implement.

The self-liquidating premium, if used correctly, can be an effective sales promotion tool for the modern sales promotion manager. It seems to work best for parity products, particularly in very competitive situations, where self-service merchandising is used.

Introduction

115

An exciting self-liquidating premium offer on the package can help the product stand out from competition not only in media advertising but at the point-of-purchase. Although the self-liquidating premium is considered a low-pressure promotion—that is, there is no strong incentive for the consumer to take advantage of the offer except the desire for the premium itself—it can work extremely well if the premium is carefully selected. One key to a good self-liquidating premium is to offer something that is not available in any other way. Thus, the only method for the consumer to obtain the premium is through the promotion offer. More and more marketers are finding that exclusive items, especially if they are fashionable or trendy, work very well. As a rule-of-thumb, the price of self-liquidating premiums must be at least 30 to 50 percent lower than the normal or expected retail price to be very successful with consumers.

The Advantages

In addition to the low cost to the marketer, ease of handling, and some protection against loss, self-liquidating premiums also offer the following advantages:

1. They can be used to extend the brand image. A product that is sold primarily with an emotional appeal can use a self-liquidating premium to extend and enhance that image. For example, Marlboro cigarettes has done an excellent job of extending its "western" advertising theme with self-liquidating premiums tied to the Old West. (See Figure 9-1.)
2. Self-liquidating premiums can also be used to reinforce the advertising campaign. Products and premiums tied to an advertising character, spokesman, or theme can be quite effective. For example, Green Giant Company has used self-liquidating premiums for years to build recognition of its brand. In one campaign, Green Giant offered a sleeping bag for two proofs-of-purchase and a check for $8.95. "Bedtime is a ho-ho-whole lot of fun," the ad stated, "with your own Little Sprout Sleeping Bag." The Little Sprout, a continuing character in Green Giant advertising, appeared on the bag itself in a number of characteristic poses, including sleeping. (See Figure 9-2.)
3. Studies have shown that self-liquidating premiums can increase advertising readership, sometimes by as much as 50 percent. If the product is of normally low interest, a self-liquidating premium used in the media advertising can help get the advertising read and the message across.
4. In many instances, the self-liquidating premium offer can be set up so that there is no actual investment in the sales promo-

FIGURE 9-1. Self-Liquidating Premium: Marlboro Cigarettes

Source: William A. Robinson, *Best Sales Promotions of 1977/78* (Chicago: Crain Books, 1979), p. 99.

tion plan except the advertising necessary to support the program. Of course, this type of program can be done only with very general premiums that may or may not have widespread appeal.

5. Premiums can be selected or offered that are of special interest to selected groups. Thus, you can actually target your sales promotion program to a specific demographic or psychographic group simply by the choice of the premium. For example,

FIGURE 9-2. Self-Liquidating Premium: Green Giant Products
Source: Robinson, *Best Sales Promotions of 1977/78*, p. 102.

FIGURE 9-3. Self-Liquidating Premium: Gatorade Drink

Source: Robinson, *Best Sales Promotions of 1977/78*, p. 93.

Gatorade used a squeeze bottle similar to the type used by sports teams to appeal to young athletes. (See Figure 9-3.)

6. By using a multiple proof-of-purchase requirement for a self-liquidating premium, sales of the product can often be encouraged.

7. Self-liquidating premiums can be used by the sales force to get store displays. If the premium is exciting, the trade may be willing to give the product additional support at very low cost to the marketer. A highly desirable product can often be used as a dealer loader—a sample given to the dealer to encourage him to stock the product.

8. Premiums can be used to reward present users and thus build brand loyalty. Quaker Oats used cookie jars for this purpose, as Figure 9-4 illustrates.

9. Self-liquidating premium offers can increase coupon redemption up to 3 or 4 percent when the coupon and premium are offered in the same promotion.

FIGURE 9-4. Self-Liquidating Premium: Quaker Oats Cereal
Source: Robinson, *Best Sales Promotions of 1977/78*, p. 87.

While self-liquidating premiums may appear to be very attractive, one should keep their disadvantages in mind. In particular, a retailer will resist putting emphasis behind a self-liquidating premium that competes with other products he sells. For example, if a discount store sells woolen blankets, the store manager won't get very excited about a self-liquidating premium that offers the same blanket at a discount or reduced price to their customers. In addition:

The Disadvantages

1. Self-liquidating premiums don't usually build trial for a product. The premium must be extremely strong to encourage new users to purchase the product. Usually, self-liquidators are more effective in holding present customers or rewarding them for past purchases.
2. Self-liquidators don't have widespread appeal. It's estimated that less than 10 percent of the population have ever sent away for a self-liquidating premium.
3. They don't develop much activity for the brand. While they may have great appeal to some groups, redemption of self-liquidating premiums is usually less than 1 percent of the media circulation where it is offered.
4. Self-liquidators can be quite expensive, particularly if the item is exclusive or developed especially for one advertiser. For example, many premium suppliers require that a commitment be made for a specific quantity of self-liquidating premiums, particularly if they are to be personalized with the brand name or logo or in some other manner. Sometimes the manufacturer must commit for a very large quantity in order to obtain a favorable price. Then, if the premiums don't redeem well, he is stuck with them.
5. To be successful, a self-liquidator must usually be advertised in the media. Self-liquidators are not particularly strong as off-shelf promotion devices. Therefore media must be used to generate interest. Often that same amount of money, invested in some other form of sales promotion, can generate more dramatic sales results.
6. The handling of self-liquidator redemptions may be poor. Slow delivery, loss in the mail, misplaced orders, and the like are potential hazards. Since a self-liquidating premium involves money, consumers get more upset about poor handling with this sort of premium than they do with other offers such as free-in-the-mail.

Some Guidelines

Since there are literally thousands of self-liquidating premium offers made each year, information about them is more complete than in other areas of sales promotion. If you're considering a self-liquidating premium, the following points are critical.

Costs

Technically, self-liquidating premium offers can be made with little or no cost to the marketer. Manufacturers often make their products available to the advertiser at substantial discounts. If the cost of the product, as well as handling, fulfillment, and postage, are included in the price to the consumer, the advertiser has actually invested only in advertising and promotion.

If the premium is to be personalized or if a product is developed specifically for the advertiser, the premium supplier usually requires commitment to a quantity. This is essentially a guarantee that so many of the premiums will be bought by the advertiser, regardless of the number of orders he receives. If the number redeemed exceeds the commitment, the marketer has no liability. If, however, orders don't exceed the commitment, the advertiser is then liable for the balance of the stock. For example, assume you have agreed to commit for 5,000 specially imprinted beach towels at a cost of $2 each. You offer the self-liquidating premium at $3, to cover the cost of the beach towel plus postage and handling. As a result of the offer, 3,500 towels out of the 5,000 commitment are ordered. You are still responsible to the supplier for the additional 1,500 towels at $2 each. Some organizations buy unused premiums but usually at a large discount. Because such promotions can be highly expensive propositions if the premium is costly and there is no consumer interest, most premiums are tested in some fashion before any commitment is made.

In addition to the cost of the premium, other costs normally incurred in a self-liquidating premium offer are:

- Media advertising, whether manufacturer originated or co-op.
- Promotional materials, such as posters, mail-in coupons, banners, displays, and other in-store materials.
- Additional handling or fulfillment not covered by the amount sent in by the consumer.

Premium Value

Traditionally, self-liquidating premiums have been thought of as rather low-cost items. But that has changed dramatically in the past few years. Marketers have learned that just about any desirable item can be liquidated—if the offer is right, if there is sufficient promotion behind it, and if it is wanted and desired by the consumer. The cost of the item is usually the major consideration. But what is really important is the value offered. Self-liquidating premiums with the retail value stated seem to redeem best. The rule-of-thumb for a successful offer is that the liquidating price must be at least 30 to 50 percent below the normal retail price. Generally, most self-liquidators are in the $3 to $10 (to the consumer) range, although that figure is gradually creeping upward.

Premium value can often be increased by using items that are exclusive or distinctive. If the item is not available in retail stores, it often has more appeal than those items that are readily available.

The real key to a successful self-liquidating premium promotion is in the care with which the item is selected, based on its appeal to consumers.

Timing

There really doesn't seem to be any specific timing consideration with self-liquidating offers. They work well in any season of the year. Also, it is fairly easy to get a self-liquidating premium into the market. The only variables are the lead time necessary for the advertising and the availability of the product to be liquidated. Since the offer can be started at any time, many marketers have standard self-liquidators that they hold in reserve for varying market conditions. A major advantage of this type of promotion is that it can also be stopped at any time. The only requirement is that orders in process be completed.

Premium Selection

It makes little sense to spend advertising money in support of a premium with little or no appeal. Therefore, we strongly suggest that all premiums be pretested in some fashion. We also suggest that premiums be related to the product, to maximize interest and action. Finally, they should be selected for their ability to create trade interest and off-shelf display rather than for number of anticipated returns received or premiums liquidated.

Response

While the traditional method of evaluating a self-liquidating premium offer has been the number of orders filled, we don't believe this is an accurate measure of the success or failure of this sales promotion technique. Objectives set for the sales promotion program in the planning stage should be the basis for evaluation, not the number of premiums redeemed. No one really cares how many premiums are moved except the premium supplier.

As a general guide, self-liquidating premiums normally don't achieve orders of much over 1 percent of the gross circulation of the advertising media where the offer appears. For example, if the offer is made in magazines with a total combined circulation of 2,000,000 copies, then returns from the self-liquidator would be expected to be in the neighborhood of 20,000. Some offers run well ahead of that mark and some well below it. It depends a great deal on the premium itself, the audience, the price of the product, and the value of the offer.

A key point in any offer is to give complete specifications about the premium in all advertising material. Give sizes, colors, and other details to help consumers visualize what they are ordering.

Some Examples

While self-liquidating offers vary greatly in methods and objectives, we believe they can be classified into seven major types, all of which are described in the next few pages.

Extend the Advertising Theme

Premiums are often used to help support the advertising theme. An excellent example is the tennis sweater offer made by Virginia Slims cigarettes. Just one of a number of self-liquidators the company has used, this one reinforced the general theme used in Virginia Slims' advertising. The slogan "You've come a long way, baby" was embroidered across the front of the sweater, along with a cartoon sketch of an old-fashioned woman tennis player—for $9 and the bottoms from two packs of regular or mentholated cigarettes. Similarly, Tab diet cola offered a drinking glass in the shape of an hour glass to complement its appeal to weight-conscious consumers: "Now you can keep your hour-glass figure with our Hour Glass." For only $3 and no proofs-of-purchase, Tab sent four 16-ounce glasses adorned with the product logo in large letters and the promotional imperative "Enjoy."

Tie-in with a Fad or Craze

Often, a self-liquidator can be found that either starts or follows a trend. While this method can be tricky, it can also be very successful. An example of this type of premium is the offer made a few years ago by Viva towels when the L.E.D. watch was new and very popular (Figure 9-5).

Tie-in with the Product

If the self-liquidating premium can be related to the product in some way, it helps to build the value of the entire sales promotion program. A good example is a premium that encourages the use of the product in some way or that can be used with the product. Nestlé found several premiums that could be directly related to its instant tea, from things that help cause a thirst to things that help cure it (Figure 9-6). The Tab "Hour Glass" promotion also fits into this category.

FIGURE 9-5. Self-Liquidating Premium: Viva Towels

Source: William A. Robinson, *100 Best Sales Promotions of 1976/77* (Chicago: Crain Books), p. 79.

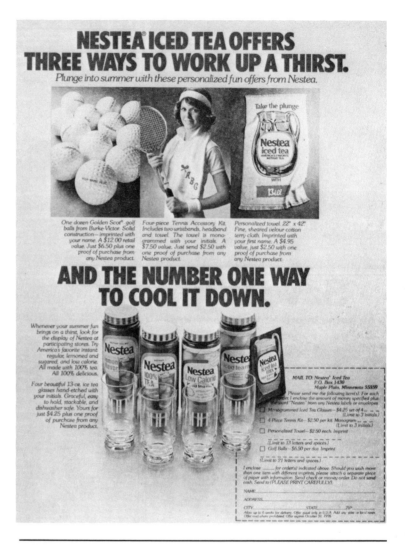

FIGURE 9-6. Self-Liquidating Premium: Nestea Iced Tea
Source: Robinson, *100 Best Sales Promotions of 1976/77*, p. 81.

Extend the Use of the Product or Package

As we said before, if the premium suggests ways to extend the use or reuse of the advertised product, that greatly increases its effectiveness as a premium. Mateus wine developed a self-liquidating premium idea that involved the use of their empty wine bottles as parts of a cruet set (Figure 9-7). Not only was it a unique idea for the extended use of the product package; the consumer was reminded of Mateus each time the set was used.

The Mateus Cruet Set Only $3.95

The perfect way to cap off your little 6.1-oz. empty bottles of Mateus.

© 1976 Imported by Dreyfus-Ashby & Co., N.Y., N.Y.

Up 'til now, there wasn't much you could do with your cute mini-bottles of Mateus, once the Mateus disappeared. (Except maybe stare at them and wonder what in the world you could do with them.)

But no more. Now you can turn those little bottles of wine into big bottles of other tasty things. Like salt. And pepper. And salad dressing.

All it takes is the Mini-Mateus Cruet Set. You get everything you need. Six attractive labels (Salt, Pepper, Oil, Vinegar, French, Italian). Four snap-on spouts. And a handsome butcher block serving stand, to boot. All for just $3.95.

The Mini-Mateus Cruet Set. Order one today.

It's the perfect way to cap off your little empty bottles of Mateus.

MATEUS WHITE ROSE MATEUS

Gentlemen:
Please send me_____set(s).
Enclosed is a check (or money order)
for_____@ $3.95 per set.
Allow 5 weeks for delivery.

Mail to: SHAPECRAFT CORP.
P.O. Box 2018
Hillside, N.J. 07205

Name_____

Address_____

City_____State_____Zip_____

(Offer good only where permitted.)

FIGURE 9-7. Self-Liquidating Premium: Mateus Wine

Source: Robinson, *100 Best Sales Promotions of 1976/77*, p. 87.

Offer Several Premiums

The premium offer can be enhanced through the use of multiple self-liquidating premiums. If one item doesn't appeal, another might. Often, these are set-building or related-item offers. An excellent example of this type of premium was made by Sunkist lem-

FIGURE 9-8. Self-Liquidating Premium: Kool Cigarettes
Source: Robinson, *100 Best Sales Promotions of 1976/77*, p. 93.

ons: a "Lemon-Aid Kit" that included a grater, a juicer, a faucet, two "snackers" (peelers), and a lemon-recipe book—a $3.10 value for $2. Each tool was also available individually at the face-value price. Clairol offered "The Nice 'n Easy Wardrobe"—slicker, umbrella, tote bag, and T-shirt (all monogrammed and the latter three in at least two different colors)—at 40 to 50 percent off the retail value with 4 proofs-of-purchase. Coca Cola tied-in with the summer sports season by offering balls for eight different sports at up to 75 percent below "suggested retail" and proofs-of-purchase from two six-packs or large bottles of Coke. The variety appealed to the two primary markets for the product, teenagers and young adults.

Use the Brand Name or Logotype

Perhaps one of the best ways to help extend the advertising image or remind the consumer of the brand is through a self-liquidating premium that carries the package design, the logotype, or the brand name. Campbell soup has done a great job of extending its brand and its package design with all sorts of effective premium offers. One of the best was the soup thermos, designed to look like the Campbell soup can. Quaker Oats cereal offered a cookie jar modeled on the product package. Diet Rite cola advertised a "trucker's shirt" with the product label affixed front and back. And Brown & Williamson promoted 21 different items, including bathing suits, sun visors, bedsheets, and tote bags—all imprinted with the Kool label, the Kool logo, or both.

Use High-Value Premiums

Several years ago, almost everyone in sales promotion would have agreed there was no way to liquidate a premium selling at over $100, much less $600. That, of course, was before Kool cigarettes made its catamaran offer (Figure 9-8). Now, almost anything can be liquidated, from doghouses to diamond rings.

While we could offer many more examples of successful self-liquidators, these items should indicate what we feel is important in such an offer. The premium should have a reason for being. It should extend or improve the overall image of the product or remind the user of the brand. That, and not the number of premiums redeemed, is the way to evaluate a self-liquidating premium offer.

Refunds

Probably the hottest sales promotion technique in the 1980s will be the refund offer. As more and more shoppers seek methods of stretching their available budget in inflationary times, the refund has more and more appeal. For example, a study conducted by Manufacturer's Marketing Services shows that the number of U.S. households using refund offers increased from 34 percent in 1978 to 59 percent in 1979. Nielsen Clearing House reported that 74 percent of all households were aware of refunds, with the average household getting four refunds per year.[1] These figures show how important refund offers are to the sales promotion manager today.

Quite simply, a refund promotion is an offer by a manufacturer or a marketer to refund a certain amount of money when the product is purchased alone or in combination with some other product or products. Refunds may range from a small percentage of the retail price of the product to the full amount. In addition, a refund may be made on the purchase of companion products in the line or on another product that is commonly used with the purchased brand. There is literally no limit to the ways in which refund offers can be made. We'll illustrate several of them in this chapter.

While refund offers have many purposes, based on the objectives of the company, the primary ones seem to be (1) to obtain trial of the product, (2) to provide a continuity-of-purchase incentive, (3) to reward loyal customers so that they will remain loyal, and (4) to "load" customers and pre-empt competitive activities. Refund offers seem to work well in obtaining product trial. For example, if the consumer knows that there is no risk in trying the product and

Introduction

---

[1]Louis J. Haugh, "Cash Refunds Multiply," *Advertising Age*, May 5, 1980, p. 48.

that the purchase price will be refunded, there is much more incentive to try a new product or a new brand. From the marketer's viewpoint, the technique works well because it is tied directly to the purchase. If the consumer buys, the refund is made. Therefore, the marketer is actually paying a certain price to obtain trial of the product. This is a *guaranteed* trial, as opposed to trial-*inducing* promotions, such as media advertising.

While the refund offer originated in the food business, makers of drugs, health and beauty products, hard goods, appliances, and automobiles—and even some service organizations—are now using it. It seems that a good idea is a good idea everywhere.

Since refund offers seem to work best in generating trial, they are naturally widely used with new products. They are also most effective in competitive situations in which the products are considered to be at parity. When there appears to be little difference between brands in the market or on the shelf, the refund offer may sway the purchase decision. In addition, refunds seem to work very well for products with a low brand share. Since the consumer is using a product in the category and there is little apparent difference between brands, the decision to try a lesser known or less well accepted brand can be justified by the refund offer. Refund offers are also effective for products moving into new geographic areas or attempting new distribution patterns.

While refund offers can be made on almost all types of products, some products and product categories seem to respond better than others. Experience suggests that refunds work best on slow-moving, parity-type, impulse products that are purchased rather infrequently but tend to be used up quickly once purchased. They do not seem to work as well on highly personal products or those that are used sparingly over time.

Types

Some manufacturers have offered a refund on the full purchase price of their product, but this can be done only on relatively low-priced products. An increasing number of marketers are offering a fixed dollar value as the refund instead. This method solves several problems: (1) it allows higher-priced products to set a reasonable refund figure; (2) it enables the sales promotion manager to estimate the cost of the refund more accurately than he could if the refund were tied to a fluctuating purchase price; (3) it is easier for the consumer to understand; and (4) it is easier to handle logistically (no check on retail prices, no calculating amounts, etc.).

Although there are many different kinds of refund offers, the most common fall into four categories, all of which are illustrated below.

Purchase of One Product

Because refunds under $1 are fairly rare, most refunds are offered
for multiple purchases, especially for low-priced package goods. Refunds for single purchases are generally confined to considered-pur-
chase goods or higher-priced food and drug products, household
items, and health and beauty aids. At the high end, automobile
manufacturers have offered $500 and even $1,000 refunds on the
purchase of new cars. More modestly (and more typically), makers
of package goods, such as Butterball turkeys (Figure 10-1), pay $1
or $2 refunds in exchange for one proof-of-purchase. The purchaser
of one Butterball turkey was also sent a $1 coupon for mailing in
additional material. More often, however, coupons are available
with the mail-in certificate printed in the ad.

FIGURE 10-1. Refund: Purchase of One Product

Source: William A. Robinson, *100 Best Sales Promotions* (Chicago:
Crain Books, 1980), p. 115.

Multiple Purchase of One Product

Many refunds are made on two or more purchases of a single product. Snow Crop, for example, offered varying refunds, based on the number of purchases of its orange juice (Figure 10-2). Buy 3, get 50¢. Buy 6, get $1. Buy 12, get $2. Sanka coffee refunded $1 for 12 empty coffee envelopes, and $2 for seals from two 8-ounce coffee jars. Grant's scotch whiskey offered $3 in return for three labels from its quart bottles.

FIGURE 10-2. Refund: Multiple Purchase of One Product

Source: William A. Robinson, *100 Best Sales Promotions of 1976/77* (Chicago: Crain Books, 1977), p. 113.

Purchase of Several Products from One Manufacturer

Refunds can also be made on the purchase of different products from the same manufacturer. Figure 10-3 shows examples of this type of offer from Clairol, Franco-American, and Nabisco. Usually, a purchase of six items is the limit, but Rival dog food offered $2.50 for nine different labels. Most companies with a great variety of products, such as Birds Eye and Johnson & Johnson, allow the

FIGURE 10-3. Refund: Purchase of Several Products from One Manufacturer

Source: "Chips Ahoy" Refund Coupon reprinted with permission of Nabisco, Inc.; "Clairol" coupon courtesy of Clairol; Inc., "Franco-American" coupon courtesy of Franco-American.

consumer to choose a relatively small number of products to qualify for the refund.

Purchase of Related Products

Refunds on go-together products are another popular approach. For example, a dairy company and a bread manufacturer might jointly offer a refund on cheese when their two products are purchased together. Or a chocolate drink marketer might offer 50¢ toward the purchase of milk when his product is purchased. This type of offer is limited only by the imagination of the sales promotion manager and the amount of money that can be invested in the promotion. An example of this type of offer is shown in Figure 10-4.

The Advantages

Refund offers have increased in popularity tremendously in the past few years. Here are some of the reasons why.

1. Refunds can build excitement for a brand at a relatively low cost. Since redemption of refund offers is relatively low, usually only about 1 percent of the media circulation of the offer, a fairly substantial offer can be made and the cost still remain within reason for the marketer. As inflation increases, however, the redemption rate has been rising, too.
2. Refund offers help build brand loyalty. The multiple purchase requirement on most offers helps to load the consumer and build brand loyalty. Consumers usually like the offers since they are a form of reward.
3. A high value offer can be made with a refund, yet the refund redemption cost to the manufacturer may be very low. The 1 percent of media circulation results because many consumers initially respond to the offer by purchasing the product but never get around to sending for the refund. This is called "slippage," which simply means that a number of people who started to save for the refund never claimed it. According to Nielsen Clearing House, 17 percent of those who start saving proofs frequently fail to send them in, 30 percent occasionally fail, 20 percent seldom fail, and 33 percent never fail.[2] In cases in which redemption doesn't occur, the marketer gains the sale because of the promotion, but the refund redemption cost is zero.
4. Often, a refund offer will encourage the consumer to trade up to a higher-priced brand or a larger size of the product. Since the refund appears to be an offer of something for nothing and

---

[2]Haugh, "Cash Refunds Multiply," p. 48.

FIGURE 10-4. Refund: Purchase of Related Products

Source: Reproduced courtesy of General Foods Corp., owner of
the registered trademarks SHAKE 'N BAKE® and MINUTE® Rice.

there is no apparent risk, the consumer may spend the extra
money to move up to the higher-cost product.

5. The refund offer can differentiate the product at the point-of-
   purchase. With a label "flag," the product can be made to
   stand out from other brands on the shelf. The offer itself is a
   differentiating feature and can often generate impulse purchases.

6. Occasionally, the refund offer can be used to load the consumer with product as the season is ending. For example, a refund
   offer might encourage a consumer to purchase an extra gallon

of antifreeze in the spring, even though the product might not be used until the following winter. Since part of the purchase price will be refunded and the product will keep in storage, the promotion can still be appealing.

7. When the refund is presented with enough impact, it is often possible to get off-shelf displays. A major refund offer, particularly if it is combined with some other type of sales promotion activity, can get the needed display in retail stores because it offers the consumer a real value and will move merchandise for the retailer.

8. Like so many other sales promotion techniques, the refund offer gives the sales force something to talk about with the trade. An impressive offer can generate strong sales force enthusiasm.

The Disadvantages

The basic disadvantage of the refund offer is that it often rewards present users rather than building new sales. Since these customers are already using the product, the promotion will be a price reduction rather than a sales promotion incentive program unless usage is increased in some way. In addition, refund offers have these disadvantages.

1. Low consumer interest is a major problem. While some consumers will always be interested in a refund offer, the number is usually rather small. Part of the problem may be the requirement of saving several proofs-of-purchase or the lack of immediacy in receiving the savings.

2. Refund offers often don't generate trial of the product among users who already are brand loyal. Although the offer of a purchase price refund ought to encourage trial of the product, it doesn't always happen. It is difficult to develop sufficient incentive to motivate nonusers or those who are brand-loyal to another product.

3. A major problem with refund offers is that some consumers send proofs-of-purchase from products they already have on hand—they simply clip them from products already purchased. In these cases, no sales increase is generated, and the refund actually amounts to a discount on products already sold.

4. With most refund offers, there is no immediate product movement or increase in sales. Because the offer requires several purchases, the promotion technique takes time to have an effect. If you are seeking an immediate sales increase, refunds aren't normally the answer.

5. Results of refund offers are hard to measure. While you know the number of refunds returned to the consumer, it is very difficult to trace new sales directly to this promotion vehicle. Since it works over time, the opportunity to see increases isn't very great.
6. The difficulty of getting the proof-of-purchase off the container sometimes discourages participation in the program. When planning a refund offer, be sure the required proofs-of-purchase can be easily obtained from the package or product.
7. Since the refund has no immediate impact at the retail level, retailers usually prefer some other type of sales promotion technique.

Some Guidelines

Generally, refund offers are planned and carried out by the sales promotion manager or the sales promotion department, with the exception of the fulfillment of the offer (the return of the refund). The promotion itself is not difficult to set up and can be initiated rather quickly. Quite often it is used to offset competitive activities, particularly on the local level. Since refund offers can be expensive and the refund amount can be fairly large, a good control system over the technique is a must.

When to Use

Typically, refund offers work best in product areas in which there is little promotion activity or in product categories in which there is not a constant barrage of sales promotion offers or media advertising. They do not seem to work very well in highly active promotion categories or where there is large volume and fast turnover as with detergents or coffee.

Refunds are an excellent method of offsetting competitive sales promotion tactics. They seem to work particularly well against coupons or other low cash-value promotions. The offer of a substantial amount of money as a refund is a strong factor at the point-of-purchase. Refund offers that combine several brands or categories can make a rather substantial offer to the consumer. Since slippage is usually quite high in this type of activity, the risk is worth it.

Redemption

Traditionally, redemption of refund offers has been about 1 to 2 percent of the media circulation of the offer. For example, if the refund offer were made in newspapers with a combined circulation of 1,000,000, then total refunds paid out should not exceed 10,000 to 20,000. Refund response rates vary by media, however. Nielsen has reported that the average cash refund redeems at 0.5 percent in print, 2.5 percent in point-of-purchase, and 3.8 percent if offered in-pack or on-pack. Manufacturer's Marketing Services reports that tear-off pad redemption is 1.04 percent; neck hangers, 1.01 percent; magazines, 0.65 percent; and Sunday supplements, 0.64 percent. Of course, all of these vary by offer.[3]

Redemption is always influenced by the attractiveness of the offer to the consumer and the amount of consumer interest in refunds. For example, Nielsen found that 27 percent of those surveyed by telephone in 1977 had sent in for a refund at some point in time and 17 percent in the last year. Of those who sent in for refunds, 68 percent redeemed from one to three refunds per year; 21 percent, four to six per year; and 11 percent, seven or more per year.[4]

It does appear that redemption can be increased with the use of other sales promotion techniques. For example, if point-of-purchase material is used in addition to the media advertising for the refund offer, redemption will climb to 5 or 6 percent of circulation. If a burst or feature about the refund is added to the package, redemption can climb as high as 12 percent. Depending on what you want to accomplish with the refund offer, the use of additional exposure can make a dramatic difference in results.

One of the major advantages of the refund offer is its flexibility. You can actually increase or decrease the number of refunds made by varying three factors:

1. You can raise or lower the value of the refund offer. If you are using a refund of the purchase price, activity can be increased by offering twice the purchase price. Of course, lowering the refund value reduces redemptions.
2. You can raise or lower the number of proofs-of-purchase required. By increasing the number, you reduce redemptions. By lowering the requirements, you increase them.
3. By varying the ways you advertise the offer, you can increase or decrease the number of refunds.

Fulfillment

A major factor in a successful refund offer program is the fulfillment procedure. Usually this is best handled by a fulfillment organization set up to handle redemption programs of this sort. A list of fulfillment houses can be found in Appendix II.

Typical costs for a refund offer fulfillment in 1981 were approxi-

---

[3]Haugh, "Cash Refunds Multiply," p. 48.
[4]Haugh, "Cash Refunds Multiply," p. 48.

mately $115 per thousand replies received. The advertiser pays the fulfillment organization on the basis of the number of replies to the offer received and filled as a result of the promotion. For example, let's assume advertiser Jones offers a $1 cash refund for three proofs-of-purchase of his regular product. The consumer sends the three proofs along with a coupon, giving his or her name and address to the fulfillment organization. The fulfillment organization checks the number of proofs included, to make sure they are correct. If they are, the $1, usually in cash, is then returned to the consumer. The fulfillment organization bills the advertiser for the actual number of orders filled, i.e. if 20,000 are received, the fulfillment organization bills the advertiser $2,300 ($115 per thousand × 20,000 responses) for the service. In most cases, the fulfillment house would be responsible for the cost of the return card, envelope, and addressing of the refund. The postage might or might not be included, depending on the rate used. The advertiser would, of course, be responsible for and provide the fulfillment house with the $20,000 in refunds sent back.

A major decision in a refund offer is whether to refund by cash, check, or coupon. Cash or check is traditionally the easiest method since there are no follow-up costs. When a coupon is used as the refund, an additional cost is typically incurred, since the retailer who handles the coupon is paid a handling fee and there is also a clearing house charge. Traditionally, refunds of 35¢ or less have been made in cash, while those over 35¢ have been made by check.

Costs

In addition to the value of the refund itself, several other costs are incurred in a refund offer. These include:

- Media advertising to suport the offer.
- Point-of-purchase materials, order pads, or other display materials for use at retail.
- Handling fees by the fulfillment house. This includes postage, envelopes, labor, etc.
- If a coupon is used, the clearing house fees on the handling, plus the usual handling fee to the retailer.

To estimate the cost of a refund offer, first determine the actual costs involved, including additional handling or other fees, and then calculate that against the estimated return. For example, assume you are making a purchase price refund on a package of rice that retails at 69¢. In addition to the refund price of 69¢ the fulfillment organization would charge approximately $115 for each 1,000 refunds received and returned, plus the cost of postage and supplies (envelopes, forms, etc.).

Rules

Perhaps the most important factor in presenting the refund offer is making the rules clear. State clearly how many proofs-of-purchase are required. Tell exactly what will be accepted as a proof-of-purchase. Make the order blank clear and complete. In Figure 10-5, you'll find a sample of what we consider to be a good form for making the refund offer.

Get Up To $3.00 Back

Get $3.00 for proof-of-purchase from each of the five participating brands.
Get $2.00 for proof-of-purchase from any combination of five participating brands.

Send this completed certificate and the proofs-of-purchase as specified opposite the brand to:

> Clairol Spring Savings Spree
> P.O. Box 14218
> Baltimore, Maryland 21268

Please Indicate Your Refund Category $3.00 ☐ $2.00 ☐
☐ I have indicated on the reverse side the number of proofs-of-purchase enclosed for each brand.

Name_____

Address_____

City_____State_____Zip_____
                                                    (must be included)

Limit one refund per household. Offer void where taxed, prohibited or restricted. Allow 6-8 weeks for delivery. Offer expires August 31, 1980. Offer is good only in U.S.A. and from APO/FPO box numbers. This offer is not redeemable at your store. Certificate may not be mechanically reproduced.

- -

SAVE THIS PART OF YOUR CERTIFICATE FOR YOUR RECORDS

On_____ I sent_____proofs-of-purchase required by Clairol, plus a completed certificate to Clairol Spring Savings Spree, P.O. Box 14218, Baltimore, Maryland 21268.

Dear Customer:
If you have complied with the terms of this offer, we gratefully accept and will do our best to fill it promptly. However, sometimes things go wrong despite our best efforts. If this happens, please accept our apology and address any inquiries about this offer to Clairol Spring Savings Spree, P.O. Box 14220, Baltimore, Maryland 21268. Please allow 6-8 weeks for delivery. This offer is not redeemable at your store.

FIGURE 10-5. Refund: Making the Rules Clear
Source: Courtesy of Clairol, Inc.

New Looks in Refunds

While the standard cash refund is still the most popular approach, several new ideas have recently developed. For example, a cash and coupon offer, such as a $1 refund and two 50¢ coupons (good on later purchases) gives the marketer an opportunity to make a larger claim in the headline, such as "$2 Back." It also helps build multiple purchases and seems to work quite well, since the bounceback coupons often redeem at 80 percent or more.

Another new idea is to combine a refund with a sweepstakes and even make the refund the official entry blank. There are some legal restrictions here, and an alternative method of entry must also be made available. Refund forms themselves offer promotional opportunities. For example, they can be made payable to the retailer where the original purchase was made. Some marketers have used celebrities to sign the refund check to give it some additional appeal as an autograph.

The number of proofs-of-purchase required obviously has an effect on redemption and slippage. A Nielsen Clearing House survey found that 39 percent of consumers surveyed felt that three proofs were reasonable. Fifteen percent said one was enough; 24 percent said two would be right; and 23 percent said they would be willing to save four or more proofs to obtain the refund. Based on a survey of various offers, Nielsen also found that three proofs-of-purchase were by far the most frequent requirement by manufacturers.[5] Requiring more than three reduces redemption and promotion effectiveness.

A simple checklist for refund offers, developed by Manufacturer's Marketing Services suggests that marketers

- Keep the offer simple and give clear instructions.
- Require standard proof-of-purchase—nothing esoteric.
- Require the respondent's zip code.
- Allow four weeks for delivery.
- Put the expiration date in bold type and make it easy to find.
- Limit the refund to one per family.

In addition, MMS suggests a refund expiration date of three months for media offers, six months for offers made on point-of-purchase materials, and one year for on-pack or in-pack offers.[6]

Some Examples

Because refund offers vary so widely, it is difficult to say which ones work best. And whether they are successful or not depends on the objectives of the sales promotion managers. Success aside, then, the most impressive refund offers are those that depart a little from the norm. Below, we've illustrated four examples of refund promotions that broke the mold, either by combining the refund offer with another technique or by varying the refunding method.

An unusual refund is the offer by Lauder's Scotch whisky, shown in Figure 10-6. It marked one of the first refund offers ever made in the liquor category. More important, it offered both a refund to the consumer and a contribution to the Muscular Dystrophy Association.

Sometimes, the offer of a refund based on something other than

---

[5]Haugh, "Cash Refunds Multiply," p. 48.
[6]Haugh, "Cash Refunds Multiply," p. 48.

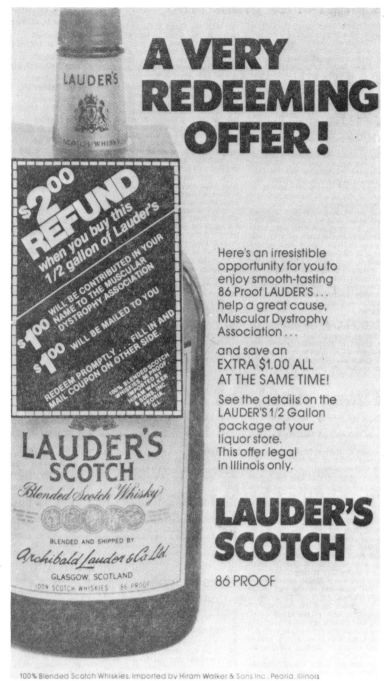

FIGURE 10-6. Refund: Lauder's Scotch Whiskey
Source: Robinson, *Best Sales Promotions of 1976/77*, p. 122.

the purchase price of the product can be very effective. While there have been many of these, one that continues to draw well is a percentage discount on grocery purchases. Actually, this kind of offer can be made for almost anything. Taster's Choice, for example, offered 10 percent off the grocery bill. (See Figure 10-7.)

FIGURE 10-7. Refund: Taster's Choice Coffee
Source: Courtesy of The Nestle Co., Inc.

Refunds on Multiple Purchases

An effective way to build up the value of the refund is to base it on multiple brands or products. Not only does this make the offer more impressive, it also allows the brands to share the cost of the promotion.

Refunds on Other Products

The refund can also be made on other products, usually those that "go with" the product being promoted. For example, cookies and milk, bread and butter, bacon and eggs, and pizza and soft drinks.

Multiple Purchases of the Brand

Another way to develop a successful refund offer is to make it good on different products from one company. This offer can work for several sizes or several flavors of a single product, or for different products under one brand.

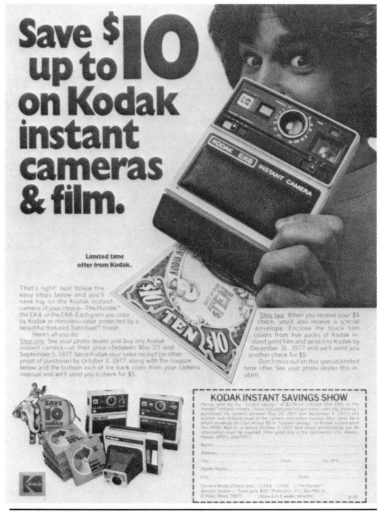

FIGURE 10-8. Refund: Kodak Camera and Film

Source: William A. Robinson, *Best Sales Promotions of 1977/78* (Chicago: Crain Books, 1979), p. 116.

To promote two of its products in a slightly different way, Kodak offered a $5 refund on its instant camera and a $5 refund on its film (Figure 10-8). The innovation was that purchasers had to buy the camera first, send in a proof-of-purchase, and then—after they received their refund on the camera—send in the covers from five packs of Kodak film in order to get the additional refund. The process was a bit complicated, but the combination enabled Kodak to advertise an appealing $10 refund offer to consumers.

To put a bit more excitement and fun into its promotion, Libby's turned a simple refund offer into a game. As illustrated in Figure 10-9, Libby's offered the consumer the opportunity to match the labels on Libby products to those on the game board, with refunds made for various combinations.

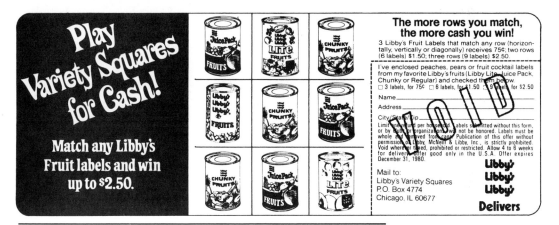

FIGURE 10-9. Refund: Libby's Products
Source: Courtesy of Libby, McNeill & Libby, Inc.© 1980.

As we have said, refunds can and have been made on nearly all types of products. Interest has grown in refund offers in the past few years, and we predict that it will soar in the future. Already, we're seeing increased retailer interest in this type of promotion, since this is one way to build sales at very little cost.

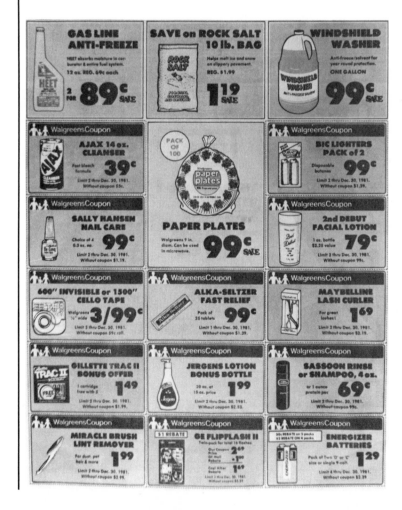

Trade Coupons

One of the most effective sales promotion devices that is almost sure to generate consumer action at the retail level is the trade coupon. The trade coupon is redeemable only at one specific retail store or chain, in contrast to a manufacturer's coupon (see Chapter 2) that can be redeemed at any retailer that stocks the product.

A trade coupon can appear in a retailer's newspaper advertisement, in a flyer, on an in-store coupon page, or banded to the product in the store. Whatever shape it takes or however it is distributed, the trade coupon represents an agreement between the manufacturer and the retailer, often in the form of some sort of allowance from the manufacturer, which permits the retailer to make the offer to the consumer through the coupon. Since the trade coupon offer is good only at the retail store at which the coupon was issued, the retailer has a strong incentive to promote it. This can be done through extra displays and in-store materials.

Usually, the manufacturer agrees to reimburse the retailer a certain amount per coupon for all the coupons redeemed. The manufacturer may redeem at full face value or less, depending on his agreement with the retailer. The retailer also often adds value to the coupon above that which the manufacturer has agreed to pay. This enables him to have a consumer leader or feature at a reasonable price. For example, assume that Manufacturer Jones agrees with Retailer Smith that a trade coupon promotion will be developed on the Jones brand. Jones offers to reimburse Retailer Smith 15¢ for each coupon received on the sale of the Jones product during a certain period. In addition, Retailer Smith decides to increase the value of the coupon to 25¢ and to cover the additional 10¢ price reduction out of his margin. Thus, Retailer Smith has developed a 25¢ off coupon that costs him only 10¢.

Introduction

149

Since the only limits on potential trade coupon redemption are the number of units of the product in the store and the number of coupons available, some manufacturers set top limits on redemptions in advance. In the above example, Manufacturer Jones might have set a limit of 2,000 coupons that he would redeem during the promotion, no matter how many coupons Retailer Smith actually accepted. The manufacturer can also limit the total dollar amount of redemption in advance by agreement with the retailer. In either case, Retailer Smith would be responsible for the full value of all coupons redeemed in excess of the number or dollar value he and Jones had agreed on. This limit is becoming more the rule than the exception, since many manufacturers want to be certain of the maximum cost of the promotion in advance.

From the manufacturer's view, the primary purpose of trade coupons is the assurance that a proposed price reduction will be passed along to the consumer. He also knows he will be paying only on actual sales and for a limited period of time. The retailer sees the trade coupon as something that can help him maintain his low-price image, give him something different from competition, and assure him that he will generate store traffic since he is often the only one with that particular coupon feature at that time.

Trade coupons seem to be particularly effective in very competitive situations. For example, a trade coupon featured by a major retailer may preclude the use of a competitive feature offered at the same time by others in the market. When this happens, competition has been blocked from retail promotion, at least for a while. Trade coupons also work well in opening new territories or introducing new products. Although consumers may not know the new brand, they certainly know the retailer. If they are regular customers, they tend to transfer acceptance from the retailer to the brand. In addition, trade coupons are a guaranteed way to get a reduced price to the consumer. Whereas other forms of mass media may or may not get the product offer out, a trade coupon, because it has a guaranteed distribution and access to the retailer's customers, is more likely to be seen and/or heard.

Types

Trade coupons can be distributed in several different ways. The most common is the in-ad coupon, which appears in the retailer's newspaper advertisement or flyer. (See Figure 11-1.)

Retailers can use trade coupons in their stores by placing them on the shelf next to the product (Figure 11-2). They can also be banded or taped to the product. No matter how they are distributed, the retailer must often collect the coupons, if only to keep a record or to give an accounting of the redemption to the manufacturer for reimbursement.

FIGURE 11-1. Trade Coupons: In-ad
Source: Courtesy of Walgreens Drug Stores.

The retailer can also use trade coupons in-store by putting them in a coupon flyer. The example shown in Figure 11-3 is typical of the trade coupons that many stores offer each week to their customers. Note that a number of manufacturers are represented, along with trade coupons from the store's own brands.

David L. Ryan of the Glendinning Promotion Group has identified five basic types of trade coupons:

1. *Discount on One Unit*—This type offers "X¢ off" the price of one unit, or features the item at "only Y¢ with coupon."
2. *Multiple-Unit Discount*—This type is often used on products normally featured in multiples, for example, "4 boxes of cake mix for $2.00 with coupon."
3. *"Get One Free" (usually with the purchase of X units)*—This is usually a very high coupon value, although products normally purchased in large multiples can offer one free using normal in-ad coupon discounts. An example would be a free bath-size bar of soap with purchase of the same size at the regular price, with coupon.
4. *Free Trade-Chosen Item with the Purchase of X Units*—This can be very powerful in obtaining trade support, but it is harder to control. For instance, a pre-Thanksgiving coupon feature of two free cans of store brand cranberry sauce with purchase of an 8-ounce jar of instant coffee. This was sponsored by the manufacturer of the coffee. Another coupon featured a free

FIGURE 11-2. Trade Coupons: On the Shelf

Source: Dominick's Finer Foods, operators of 70 high-quality, high-volume supermarkets in the Chicago-land area.

quart jar of store brand mayonnaise with purchase of one 8-ounce jar of regular coffee.

5. *Extra Stamp Coupons*—Stamp retailers often use flyers featuring a variety of couponed products. For each product purchased, the consumer will receive 25 to 100 free trading stamps. Sometimes this may amount to as many as two books of trading stamps with purchase of all the advertised items.[1]

The Advantages

From the manufacturer's view, trade coupons have several advantages.

1. Trade coupons are a good way to generate product trial. Because the area of distribution is limited, the face value can be higher than would normally be offered. In addition, the retailer will usually promote the offer with some form of in-store activity.

2. Trade coupons can generate trade cooperation, particularly in off-shelf displays. Since the retailer has a stake in the suc-

---

[1]David L. Ryan, "The Tools of Promotion," a speech given to the Association of National Advertisers, September 1973.

FIGURE 11-3. Trade Coupons: In a Flyer

Source: Dominick's Finer Foods, operators of 70 high-quality, high-volume supermarkets in the Chicago-land area.

cess of the sales promotion program, he is usually more willing to support it with displays and other in-store features.

3. Trade coupons can increase short-term sales. The trade coupon has a short life (usually three days, or a week at the most), so sales are concentrated during that period of time. That can give a definite sales bump to the product.

4. The trade coupon is a quick and flexible sales promotion device. Since the only requirement is the availability of the product and the coupon, a trade coupon can be set up very quickly with a retailer.

5. It can be used as a replacement for the price-pack. The trade coupon gives the same value to the consumer and is less difficult to implement. Retailers also like the technique better than the price-pack, which is normally available to their competition at about the same time.

6. Often, sales of the couponed item increase even after the trade coupon is no longer in effect. The device apparently reminds or calls attention to the product and helps generate later sales at regular prices.

7. From the manufacturer's point of view, trade coupons can be used to build distribution. Individual trade couponing offers can be made to retailers, although the law requires that all offers be made to all retailers in an SMSA or trade area on a proportionately equal basis. By concentrating his efforts on individual retailers who may be either understocking or not stocking at all, the manufacturer can use trade coupons to help increase or improve distribution.

8. Trade coupons can be used to reduce trade inventories on a market-by-market basis. Since the manufacturer can implement the sales promotion device wherever and whenever needed, it has great geographical flexibility.

9. The trade coupon can be used to "sell-in" a product. As an offer to reduce the price individually to retailers, a trade coupon is often effective in getting retailers to stock the product, since they know the device will help them move the merchandise out of the store.

10. From a cost standpoint, a trade coupon may offer a saving to the manufacturer. For example, if the trade coupons are redeemed directly from the retailer by the manufacturer, the cost of a clearing house charge may be avoided.

11. Trade coupons usually generate greater sales than straight manufacturer-originated coupons of the same value. Some studies have shown that they redeem twice as well: whereas manufacturer coupons redeem at the rate of 2–4 percent, trade coupons usually redeem at a 4–6 percent rate.

12. Trade coupons do well in building multiple purchase sales too. The retailer may offer 10¢ off on the purchase of one package and 20¢ off on the purchase of two, or 25¢ off on the regular package and 50¢ off on the king size.

It is obvious from the above list why trade coupons are a favorite of both manufacturers and retailers. They offer a number of sales promotion advantages which, in some cases, are not available any other way.

The Disadvantages

While it might seem from the above list that the trade coupon is the ideal sales promotion device, there are some disadvantages.

1. Misredemption is a major problem. Since the offer is made by the retailer, the manufacturer has no control over the way in which the coupons are printed, distributed, or accepted.
2. Unless there is agreement prior to the coupon offer, it is difficult to estimate the cost of the program. There really is no accurate way to determine how many coupons will be redeemed and thus the cost incurred, except by a top limit on redemptions in either dollars or units or based on the total product the retailer has in stock.
3. Since many consumers shop the same store day after day, there is usually a high duplication rate among prospects.
4. The device cannot be used nationally since some states and some chains do not accept or allow trade coupons. It can also interfere with regular promotional programs in the areas in which it is conducted.

Some Guidelines

Again, while each trade coupon is different, there are some common factors that apply to all.

The Mechanics of Trade Coupons

Many different methods are used in setting up and redeeming trade coupons. The usual first step is for the manufacturer's representative to call on the retailer and announce the availability of the promotion. Then the manufacturer and the retailer decide the timing, the geographical extent, and the value of the coupon to be used. Often, this sales promotion device is combined with some form of trade allowance. After the preliminary agreements are worked out, the retailer signs a contract agreeing to the promotional plan. Then the retailer runs the coupon in his regular weekly ad and redeems the coupons at the check-out, just as he would with a manufacturer coupon. Finally, the retailer sends the coupon to the clearing house and is reimbursed (just as he would be with a manufacturer's coupon, including the retailer handling charge).

There are, of course, variations on this approach. The manufacturer can redeem the coupons directly to avoid the handling charge from the retailer and/or the clearing house. When this is done, there usually is no handling charge or clearing house fee involved in the transaction. The manufacturer can decide in advance how many coupons he will redeem or how much dollar value he will pay.

Timing

Trade coupons seem to work best in building traffic for the store, particularly if the brand is a high-volume one. They also seem to work better with low-priced products that are frequently purchased. High-priced items, particularly ones with a retail price of over $2, don't respond as well to trade coupons. But whether they do or not depends a great deal on the value of the coupon.

Costs

With a trade coupon, there is no distribution cost for the manufacturer. The retailer usually pays this by running the coupon in his newspaper ad or by distributing it some other way. The only manufacturer cost is the redemption, plus any handling charges agreed upon in advance.

The best estimate of trade coupon redemption is 40 to 60 percent of the units sold. Thus if you assume that 1,000 units will be sold during the time the trade coupon is valid, and the face value of the coupon is 15¢, then the estimated liability will be $161 (1,000 units × 15¢ coupon + 7¢ handling + 3½¢ clearing house × 60 percent). You would not, however, have any control over this number. If, instead of 1,000, 5,000 were sold, your estimated liability would be $805 (5,000 × 15¢ coupon + 7¢ handling + 3½¢ clearing house × 60 percent). The liability would also increase if redemption were higher than 60 percent. If, in the first example, the redemption were 80 percent instead of 60 percent, your estimated redemption cost would be $204 instead of $161.

As we said, the manufacturer may limit the number of coupons he will redeem. For example, if it were estimated that 1,000 units would be sold and that 80 percent of those would be coupon sales and if the coupon value were 25¢, the manufacturer could agree to pay the retailer $200 maximum no matter how many coupons were redeemed (1,000 units @ 25¢ × 80 percent redemption). Note also that in this instance there is no handling or clearing house fee. There are many other variations of this type of approach.

Controls

In order to control the cost of the trade coupon program, it is usually necessary to have a written agreement with the retailer. This is, in effect, a contract that states exactly what each will do, their financial responsibility, and how the promotion will be carried out. Thus, each side knows and understands what the costs and liabilities will be. The American Association of Advertising Agencies suggests the following seven rules for setting up a trade coupon program:

1. If the coupons are to be sent in for payment, work only with a reputable clearing house. Don't allow an individual or a specific local group to be responsible for gathering or "clearing" the trade coupons from a retailer.
2. Include only one brand or size in the coupon. The broader you make the coupon, the more likely it is to be misredeemed.
3. Require specific wording on the coupon, such as brand, size, expiration date, dealer's name, and "only one per household."
4. Set a specific expiration date, usually not longer than seven days.
5. Do not allow retailers to reprint the coupon for other uses, unless there is a limit on the number to be redeemed.
6. If the trade coupon is to appear in the retailer's advertisement, require a tear sheet as proof that the trade coupon appeared in the main body of the advertisement.
7. Test first before you plan any wide-scale use of the trade coupon. Learn from the test and work the "bugs" out. Don't experiment. It can be too costly.[2]

There are no doubt other "rules" applicable to trade coupons, but these seem to be the ones that cover the most "trouble spots" for the sales promotion manager. Remember, trade coupons are just like money. Treat them the same way you would treat cash.

Some Examples

While there are many different kinds of trade coupons, most can be separated into one of three groups.

The Straight Cents-Off Coupon

The cents-off coupon simply states that it is worth X¢ off the purchase price of a specific product for a specific period of time at a specific store. A multiple unit can also be used, such as three cans of peas for $1 with coupon. (See Figure 11-4.)

The Free-Product-with-Purchase Coupon

An alternative is to have a product free with the purchase of another product.

---

[2]Sales Promotion Committee, American Association of Advertising Agencies, *Sales Promotion Techniques: A Basic Guidebook* (New York: Association of Advertising Agencies, 1978), p. 44.

FIGURE 11-4. The Cents-off Trade Coupon
Source: Courtesy of Walgreen Drug Co.

The Trading Stamp Coupon

Another alternative is to have the coupon worth a certain number of extra trading stamps. Normally, this value is determined by the retailer. For example, extra S&H Green Stamps were given on a wide variety of products by A&P in the weekly newspaper advertisement shown in Figure 11-5.

FIGURE 11-5. The Trading Stamp Coupon
Source: Courtesy of Great Atlantic & Pacific Tea Company.

Trade coupons can be an effective sales promotion tool if used properly. The preceding ideas and suggestions should help you develop a sound trade coupon program.

CHAPTER

Trade Allowances and Trade Deals

In the package-goods field, the most common sales promotion device used by manufacturers to motivate retailers is some form of trade allowance or, as it is often called, trade deal. These allowances are just what the name suggests: short-term special offers, usually in the form of a reduced selling price, which the manufacturer gives the retailer as an incentive to stock the product, feature it, or in some way cooperate in the promotion of the product at the retail level. The trade deal is also offered in an attempt to obtain a reduced retail price from the retailer.

Research has shown that more than 25 percent of all retail customers are considered regular "price-off" buyers; i.e., they purchase most products "on sale" or at what they consider to be a bargain. With this large number of consumers looking for reduced prices, you can easily see why trade deals are a very important type of sales promotion technique for both the manufacturer and the retailer.

Obviously, there is no consumer advantage to a trade deal or allowance unless the retailer decides to pass the savings along. Thus, the manufacturer who offers the retailer a case allowance (a price reduction on each case of product that the retailer buys) in hopes that the retailer will pass this reduction along by lowering the shelf price will sometimes be disappointed. The trade allowance or deal may be swallowed up by the trade, with no additional effort or performance and no reduction of the retail price. The retailer simply takes the trade deal as extra margin on the product.

To overcome this problem, many manufacturers now require some sort of "performance" from the retailer to obtain the trade allowance or deal. The retailer is required to do something at the retail level to help increase sales or to earn the allowance or deal. He

Introduction

may be required to build a display, run a price feature on the product, place retail advertising in support of the brand, or make some other concession that would justify the discount being given.

Here are some examples of trade allowances commonly made by manufacturers:

- Package goods. Manufacturers offer price reductions (usually off-invoice, that is, deducted from the bill) to persuade retailers to stock up and pass savings along to consumers. Off-shelf display, advertising, and/or price reduction may be required as proof of performance.
- Cosmetics. Manufacturers pay for their own demonstrators and sales clerks, for counter space in department stores, or for "spiffs" (extra payment for sales of specific items, in addition to regular margins) to the retailers' own clerks.
- Domestics. Manufacturers add to the price to the retailer with the understanding that the excess amount will be paid back to the store later as a "promotional allowance."
- Auto aftermarket. Manufacturers offer discounts to wholesalers, who may or may not pass them on to the retailers.
- Appliances—housewares. The retailer deducts a "promotional allowance" from the invoice and the manufacturer accepts certification that funds were spent for promotion.

While these are just some examples of how trade deals are set up, they are an indication of the wide variations of approaches trade allowances and deals may take.

Although many high-sounding objectives are often given for the use of trade deals or trade allowances, sales promotion pioneer J. O. Peckham, Sr., found that in many cases they didn't perform up to expectations in the marketplace. In Table 12-1, he lists some of the common objectives set for trade deals and then lists the generally observed marketing results.

While Peckham's results don't apply to all products, they seem to be common enough, particularly with package goods, to generate serious questions about the effectiveness of the technique. In spite of these questions, however, trade deals are here to stay and the manufacturer must learn to make the best possible use of them.

Types: No Requirements

While there may be hundreds of types of trade allowances, generally they can be classified into two major groups. The first consists of allowances in which no performance is required by the retailer. They are simply discounts given to make additional sales at the wholesale or retail level. The reseller might pass along some of these discounts to the consumer in the form of reduced prices or features, but he is not required to do so.

Objectives	Marketing Results
Attract new users	Very limited
Counter competitive inroads, particularly on a new competitive brand	Little or no change in basic trend
Increase over-all purchases by present users	Only temporary, borrows sales from future
Insure adequate shelf space	No significant change
Increase inventories at retail/ wholesale level	Good
Obtain broader distribution	Very limited deal generally sold to present retail customers
Cushion introduction of consumer price increase	Only at expense of much larger price increase later
Obtain more in-store displays	No significant change
Complement advertising	Good
Stimulate interest of the sales force	Excellent

TABLE 12-1. Promotional Objectives of Trade Deals: Established Brands on Market Five Years or More

Source: J. O. Peckham, Sr., *The Wheel of Marketing* (Scarsdale, NY: Privately printed, 1978), p. 36.

Note: In this section, to simplify the discussion, we assume that the manufacturer sells directly to the retailer with no wholesaler or distributor involved. We recognize that in most instances trade promotions are developed by the manufacturer and offered to the wholesaler, who may improve on the offer or choose not to pass some of the discount along. Rather than get into this rather complex world of multiple discounts, we have chosen to simplify the steps for the sake of clarity. If the reader understands the basic concepts of each trade allowance, adjustments can be made to fit individual product categories and the various methods of distribution.

Buying Allowance

The buying allowance is simply a discount for the purchase of the product at a certain time. For example, the manufacturer might offer the retailer a buying allowance of $1 per case for all cases purchased. However, a buying allowance is often tied to the purchase of a certain number of units. For example, the manufacturer's buying allowance of $1 per case might be allowed on all purchases if 10 or more cases are purchased at one time. Or it might apply to all cases the retailer purchases in excess of the average he purchased during the same period last year. In most instances, the allowance is either deducted from the invoice or given as a credit.

Usually, the purpose of a buying allowance is simply to gain or retain distribution or to attempt to gain a lower shelf price. Often it is used to ward off competition or to load retailers prior to an anticipated competitive trade deal. While the allowance can be instituted quickly and easily and requires no special handling by the manufacturer, the retailer is not required to promote the offer in any way or to pass the savings along to the consumer. Thus, while the objective of the manufacturer might be to obtain retail price features at the store level, the retailer may absorb the discount or allowance and take it as extra margin on the product.

Although the buying allowance is by far the most popular form of trade allowance, it often results in the least action at the consumer level.

Off-Invoice Allowance

While the buying allowance usually applies to some form of quantity discount, the off-invoice allowance normally refers to a price reduction for a certain period of time. For example, again assume that the manufacturer offers a $1 per case allowance. In this instance, however, the discount is allowed on all purchases made between March 1 and April 15. It makes no difference how many cases the retailer purchases, but the purchases must be made between those dates to earn the discount. In addition, the allowance is deducted directly from the invoice for the products. For example, if the product regularly sold for $10 per case and the retailer purchased 100 cases, the cost would be $1,000. With an off-invoice allowance, however, the manufacturer would submit an invoice for $1,000 less the $100 ($1 per case on 100 cases), making a net invoice to the retailer of $900.

Manufacturers like this sort of trade allowance simply because it is fast and easy, and the retailer understands it and is accustomed to using it. Sometimes, manufacturers can convince the retailer to offer a price discount to the consumer because of the off-invoice allowance, since the offer is for a limited period of time.

The basic promotion difficulty with the off-invoice allowance is simply that the retailer may stockpile the product at the reduced price to sell later at a greater margin. There is usually no requirement that the retailer pass the reduced price along to the consumer now or at any later time.

Free Goods

In a free goods offer, the manufacturer offers an additional "free" amount of the product with the purchase of a minimum quantity. A typical offer might be to give one case free with the purchase of 12—a "baker's dozen." Normally, the free goods offer is for a limited time and may or may not be for a one-time purchase. For example, the offer might be for the period May 1 through July 15, or it might be limited to the next order the retailer places within a certain time.

Manufacturers particularly like the free goods offer since the only cost is the product being offered. This is actually the lowest net cost discount that the manufacturer can give. Here's why. Assume the cost to manufacture the product is $5 per case, and the normal wholesale price to the retailer is $10 per case. If the offer of one free case with the purchase of 10 were made, the discount cost per case on the product sold would be only 50¢ (10 cases are sold; one free case at a cost of $5 is given in the deal; $5 ÷ 10 cases = 50¢ per case). On the other hand, a buying allowance or off-invoice allowance would normally amount to more—for example, the $1 per case allowance mentioned above. While the free goods offer in our example sounds much more impressive than the offer of 50¢ off per case, it actually amounts to the same net income to the manufacturer.

Some manufacturers also prefer the free goods allowance because it may encourage the retailer to purchase more during a specific period of time. As a result of a free goods allowance, the retailer can often be encouraged to pass part of the savings along to the consumer, since he actually receives the total selling price of the free goods as profit.

A free goods allowance is an excellent trade promotion for many types of products. It doesn't work well, however, on slow-moving items. The retailer simply won't stock up on or promote a product that sells only a few units per week.

Dating

While technically not a form of trade allowance, dating is included because it involves a form of discount or method of dealer allowance. Dating simply means that the retailer can purchase a certain amount of product now and be billed for it over a period of time. In some cases, purchases may be made now at a reduced price and shipped at a later date. For example, assume the retailer purchases $750 worth of merchandise from the manufacturer on June 1. With dating, he might pay $250 on August 1, another $250 on September 1, and the final $250 on October 1. In this way, the retailer is not obligated to pay for the merchandise in advance but can spread the payments out as the merchandise is sold in the retail store. In effect, the manufacturer is financing the purchase but at no interest.

Manufacturers like the idea of dating simply because it is a fairly inexpensive form of merchandising to the trade. It can often help them save warehousing costs because they move the product out of their plant and into the warehouse or storage area of the retailer. It is a particularly good way to move seasonal goods. For example, snow blowers may be sold and shipped to the retailer in April, May, and June with datings of October, November, and December. This allows the manufacturer to encourage the retailer to have the product on hand for the selling season, yet still allows him to maintain a reasonable production schedule. Some manufacturers, particularly those whose products are high volume and fast moving, avoid dating because they are essentially financing the retailer to sell the products. Dating can obviously become a financial problem if done to excess.

Dating is typically done on fairly high-priced, slow-moving items, such as tires, batteries, some larger appliances, and seasonal equipment and materials.

Types: with Requirements

The second type of trade allowance requires some sort of performance by the retailer to earn the discount or "deal." Usually this is an attempt on the part of the manufacturer to get the price of the product reduced at the retail level or to see that some of the trade allowance is passed along to consumers.

Cash Rebate

This is the simplest form of performance contract. The manufacturer agrees to give the retailer a cash discount of some sort (so much per case, a percentage of the total, etc.), provided the retailer does a mutually agreed-upon task. That might be simply to stock the product, increase the shelf space, or purchase and display the full line. When proof of the performance of the task is provided, the manufacturer sends the retailer a check for the amount of the discount. While the agreement may be that the cash rebate will be paid upon performance, sometimes the retailer wants the money in advance. This can create a ticklish problem for the manufacturer, particularly if the retailer is a large account.

The major advantage of a cash rebate to the manufacturer is that the retailer must perform prior to payment. This enables the manufacturer to police the offer with the retailer and make sure the agreement is complied with.

Advertising or Display Allowance

Similar to the cash rebate is the advertising or display allowance. Again, the retailer must perform some function or service to earn the discount. The difference here is that normally the discount earned is in the form of a credit memo rather than cash. Additionally, the task to be performed by the retailer usually has to do with some sort of consumer offer, such as a display, a reduced price special advertised in the newspaper, a price-off shelf feature, or the like. Usually, the advertising allowance requires the placement of space or time media to promote the product. The display requirement, on the other hand, normally involves in-store presentation of the product.

The advertising or display allowance is commonly written into a contract between the manufacturer and the retailer. As part of a contract, the advertising allowance is much easier to enforce, since the allowance need not be paid until after proof-of-performance is submitted. The proof usually consists of tear sheets of newspaper ads, copies of shelf signs, pictures of displays built, or other verification that the contract was completed.

For example, the manufacturer might give a $1.50 per case advertising allowance on a purchase, if the retailer agrees to reduce the price of the product to the consumer and promote that price reduction in his regular newspaper advertisement. Usually, there are stipulations on how the advertisement must appear; that is, it must be a certain size, must appear within the main section of the newspaper ad, must be a price reduction below normal retail, and so on. The manufacturer cannot specify the amount of the reduction since this would amount to price-fixing.

Other types of advertising or display allowance include a case or unit reduction for a feature with a shelf sign or a shelf-price reduction. Displays are usually rewarded on the basis of a flat amount per display or on a sliding scale based on the size of the display. There are literally hundreds of variations on the advertising and display allowance approach, and some are used more widely in certain product categories than others.

The usual reason for an advertising or display allowance is to encourage some sort of retail activity in the store. It is also widely used to gain or hold retailers in the distribution system or to counter competitive activity.

The advertising or display allowance is easy to set up. Since it is established by contract, most retailers perform as expected. Some retailers try to take advantage of the contract and do only the minimum required. They may, for example, build only a few displays, run only the smallest possible newspaper advertisement, or offer the smallest discount to the consumer. There is little the manufacturer can do about this if the retailer has complied with the actual terms of the contract.

Display Allowances

The display allowance is similar to the advertising or display allowance but it is tied specifically to the building of a display in the store or to special shelving of the product. While it is not widely used, it deserves to be mentioned. Display allowances may or may not include a special price feature to the consumer. With some products, simply placing the product at the end of an aisle or in an off-shelf display will generate increased sales. Again, the retailer must develop some sort of display or perform in some way in the store to be eligible for the discount.

As with the advertising and display allowance, the display allowance is often paid on the basis of a flat amount per store or display. It may also be on a sliding scale based on the size of the display. Often, too, different types of displays are paid for at different rates. For example, an end-aisle might be paid at $10 while a front of store or giant display might be worth $25. It all depends on the manufacturer and his needs and objectives.

Count and Recount Allowance

The count and recount allowance is a special type of trade deal designed primarily to get the product from the wholesaler or retailer's warehouse to the stores or to reduce inventory. The reason for this strategy is that retail stores have little space for storage. Therefore, if the product is shipped to the store, it will likely be displayed and sold.

The count and recount allowance works this way: The manufacturer agrees to pay a given sum based on the opening inventory in the store or warehouse, plus the amount of product purchased, less the ending inventory in the store or warehouse. This is usually tied to a period of time, such as 60 or 90 days. For example, assume that the product being promoted is canned applesauce. The offer the manufacturer makes is that a credit of $1.50 per case will be given on all cases moved through the store or warehouse during the June 1–July 31 period.

On June 1 a count is taken of the amount of canned applesauce in the store or warehouse. Assume it amounts to 150 cases. During the time of the promotion, the retailer buys and is shipped an additional 200 cases of canned applesauce (for a total of 350 cases). On July 31, another count of the canned applesauce is made in the store or warehouse. This count shows 65 cases are still in inventory. The retailer is thus entitled to a credit of $427.50 as shown in the chart below. The $427.50 discount is then sent to the retailer in the form of a credit memo.

Count and recount allowances are primarily used by manufacturers to flush the inventory of a new package or an improved product out of the warehouse into the retail stores or simply to encourage more retail activity on the brand. They can help solve out-of-stock problems at the retail level because they force the product onto the shelf. In addition, count and recount allowances can often be used

Opening inventory	150 cases
Purchases	+ 200 cases
Subtotal	350 cases
Less inventory on hand	− 65 cases
Entitled to credit	285 cases
Allowance per case	× 1.50
Total credit	$427.50

to help force a lower shelf price or feature on the brand at the retail store.

Manufacturers like this sales promotion technique because it is easy to institute. No shipments or sales are required to get it going. In addition, the count and recount offer is paid only on the product that is sold or moved.

Unfortunately, the retailer is not forced to act with this sort of sales promotion device. He may only increase his stock of the product at the store level and not increase sales. This type of promotion also requires a great deal of the manufacturer's sales force's time to set it up and carry it through. The biggest disadvantage to the manufacturer is that there is no incentive to restock the warehouse. In the illustration above, the warehouse stock declined from 150 cases to 65 cases. With this type of inventory, the retailer is not likely to develop any sort of promotional activity but may be content just to hold the smaller stock.

Buy-Back Allowance

In an attempt to solve the problem of restocking the store or warehouse after a count and recount allowance, a buy-back allowance may be offered. This simply consists of a "deal" to encourage bringing the store or warehouse stock level up or back to where it was prior to the time the count and recount allowance was given. It works this way.

Let's use the canned applesauce example again. At the end of the promotion period, the warehouse has only 65 cases in stock. A buy-back allowance of $1 per case might be made on enough cases to bring the stock level back to its original starting point. (In our example this would be a total of 150 cases.) An alternative is to limit the allowance to the number of cases sold during the count and recount allowance. (In the above example, this would have been 285 cases; 350 cases on hand or purchased, less 65 cases on hand at end of promotion.) If the buy back were limited to an amount intended to bring the inventory level back to the starting point, the retailer could buy a total of 85 cases (150 starting inventory minus 65 cases ending inventory) at a $1 per case discount. This would amount to a credit of $85. If the limit were the number of cases moved, the retailer could purchase 285 cases. At the discount of $1 each, this would be a total of $285. In most instances, the buy-back allowance is on a single purchase at one given time, and the discount generated is given in the form of a credit memo against the purchases made. Usually it is limited to the amount of merchandise purchased during the previous period.

Manufacturers like the buy-back allowance because it is an incentive to the dealer to restock the warehouse. Retailers like it for the same reason, since it allows them to bring their warehouse stock up to the previous level at a reduced price.

While the retailer is not required to pass any of the savings on a buy-back allowance along to the consumer, the manufacturer does have control over the promotion, and there is usually a set limit on what is offered.

Although proof-of-performance is listed in each of the above trade promotions, it is very hard to enforce. If the retailer wants to, he can cheat or totally avoid fulfilling the contract. There is little recourse for the manufacturer except to attempt better persuasion tactics in the future.

The Advantages

There are some general reasons why manufacturers use this form of trade incentive:

1. Most types of trade allowances or trade deals are effective in moving the product from the manufacturer to and through the warehouse to the retail shelf. In most product categories, the retailer is the key to increased sales. Although there may be no direct responsibility to have a consumer promotion or reduce the price on the shelf, a trade allowance to the retailer is often passed along in the form of reduced consumer prices.
2. Most trade allowances are very flexible. They can be added where needed on a market-by-market basis. In addition, they can be varied by area. By law, however, the same deal must be made available to all retailers in a given marketing area. Usually this is done on the basis of a Standard Metropolitan Statistical Area or a trading area under some other definition.
3. Trade allowances can be instituted very quickly. The only requirement is to make the offer to the wholesaler or retailer. Thus, no preparation time is required. This is an excellent tool to combat competitive activities.
4. Trade allowances can increase store volume. Even if there is no requirement to pass the offer along to the consumer, the

retailer may choose to develop a feature or a special on the product in some way, since he has an opportunity to generate increased sales at improved margins. Of course, an increase in store volume is more likely when some retailer performance is employed.

The Disadvantages

Although the manufacturer always wants to find ways to move additional product, trade allowances can become a crutch for the sales force. They become convinced that the product can't be sold unless it is on "deal." In addition, there are other disadvantages of this type of sales promotion.

1. Trade deals can be overdone. If used too often, they lose their effect with the retailer, because he comes to expect a "deal" or buys only when a special price is offered. In these instances, the regular price of the product to the retailer may be replaced by the "deal" price over a period of time.
2. Too many deals can overload the trade with the product. Since retailers like to take advantage of the reduced price opportunities, they will often overbuy or overstock. When this happens, the manufacturer may find an uneven flow of product, warehousing, or retail activity.
3. Many retailers are lax in passing the trade allowance through to the consumer. What the manufacturer may consider to be a major consumer offer or price reduction may never materialize.
4. Often, trade allowances are abused by the trade. Retailers may agree to do certain things but then fail to do some or all of them. The manufacturer has little recourse in these situations, except to stop selling to the retailer, which is not an attractive choice. Further, trade deals usually require some form of policing by the manufacturer. This can take up the time of the sales force, which could be better used in making sales calls rather than following up on trade deals.

Despite their disadvantages, trade allowances are here to stay. Manufacturers will not give them up and retailers will not stop asking for them. They are simply a way of selling the product, and as a part of the sales promotion effort they will probably continue to be used in some form or another.

Some Guidelines

Aside from the advantages and disadvantages of trade deals discussed in the last section, there are some general "rules" for the use of this promotion technique. J. O. Peckham, Sr., using A. C. Nielsen Company data, found that trade deals and allowances were most effective under the following conditions.

1. When given as payment for *added* store effort on *new items* in the form of displays, advertising or lower than normal retail price.
2. When given as payment for *added* store effort on established items such as a special store-wide sale at a special price.
3. When used only occasionally, rather than as a continuous operation.[1]

Sales Effect

Of perhaps more importance than these general rules are the sales effects of trade deals and the general economics of them. Peckham believes that the effectiveness of trade deals should be determined at the consumer level, not at the trade level. (See Table 12-2.)

Referring to the data given in Table 12-2, Peckham says,

[Here is] a simulation of the sales effect of a 10% discount of $1.00 per case on all purchases of a specific brand made by the trade over a 60-day period. Note that the first section to the left contrasts factory or manufacturer's sales over a fourteen-month period involving the trade deals as shown in the dotted lines with those of the previous "normal" year without the trade deals shown in the solid line. Case sales of this seasonal product during the first January-February bimonthly period are indexed at 100 in all cases.

Referring to the chart, during the 60-day deal period of May-June, manufacturer's sales rose to an index of 300—twice the seasonal increase obtained during the previous normal year. This was followed by eight months of sub-normal factory sales as shown by the difference between the dotted and the solid lines on the left-hand side of the chart. If we assume the same case sale starting point during both fourteen-month periods and total the index numbers representing case sales, we see that there is an apparent increase of 105 index points (cases) or 12%, indicating that the trade deals seem to produce fairly substantial results. On the other hand, if we make this analysis at the warehouse or wholesale level as shown in the center section of the chart, the increase in sales to the retail trade appears to be only 100 points (cases) or 10.6%, the difference being what still remains in warehouse stocks. Furthermore, the retailer also took advantage of the deal situation to stock up at low

---

[1]J. O. Peckham, *The Wheel of Marketing* (Scarsdale, N.Y.: Privately printed, 1978), p. 33.

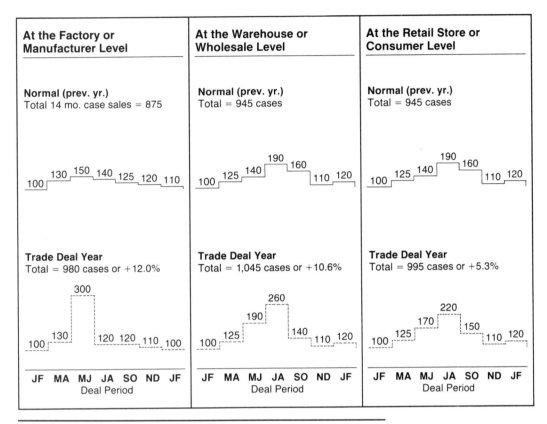

At the Factory or Manufacturer Level	At the Warehouse or Wholesale Level	At the Retail Store or Consumer Level
Normal (prev. yr.) Total 14 mo. case sales = 875	**Normal (prev. yr.)** Total = 945 cases	**Normal (prev. yr.)** Total = 945 cases
Trade Deal Year Total = 980 cases or +12.0%	**Trade Deal Year** Total = 1,045 cases or +10.6%	**Trade Deal Year** Total = 995 cases or +5.3%
JF MA MJ JA SO ND JF Deal Period	JF MA MJ JA SO ND JF Deal Period	JF MA MJ JA SO ND JF Deal Period

TABLE 12-2. Sales Effect of a 10 Percent Trade Deal (Simulated)
Source: Peckham, *The Wheel of Marketing*, p. 33.

prices and if we analyze his sales to consumers as we do in the righthand section of the chart, we see that consumer sales increased only 50 cases, or 5.3%. From the standpoint of sales movement through to the consumer, therefore, the manufacturer is really ahead only 50 cases or 5.3% during the year of the deal with the balance going into retail and wholesale stocks.

What is the economic effect of this operation as far as the manufacturer is concerned? While this is virtually impossible to determine accurately, an approximate idea can be obtained by contrasting the gross trading profit (GTP) on the *additional consumer sales* apparently resulting from the trade deal with the cost of the deal itself. In this case, the gross trading profit is that which remains when the cost of goods sold is deducted from manufacturer revenue and thus includes selling expenses, administrative expense, advertising and promotional expense, taxes and ultimate net profit. In making this analysis, it is assumed that none of these costs, with the exception of deal costs, will increase as a result of the temporary bulge in sales. It is hoped that, at the very least, the additional gross trading profit will balance the promotion costs.

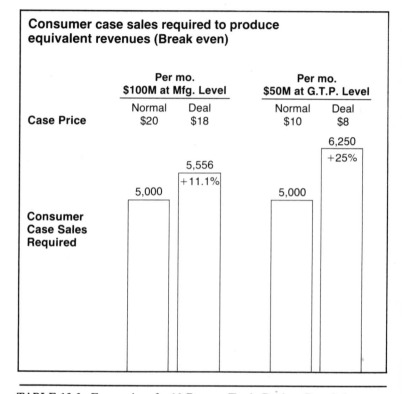

Consumer case sales required to produce equivalent revenues (Break even)

	Per mo. $100M at Mfg. Level		Per mo. $50M at G.T.P. Level	
	Normal	Deal	Normal	Deal
Case Price	$20	$18	$10	$8
		5,556 +11.1%		6,250 +25%
Consumer Case Sales Required	5,000		5,000	

TABLE 12-3. Economics of a 10 Percent Trade Deal on Branded Items Normally Selling to Trade at $20 per Case
Source: Peckham, *The Wheel of Marketing*, p. 39.

What increase in *consumer* sales would be necessary just to break even—to balance promotion costs? Table 12-3 attempts to answer this by analyzing the economics of a 10% trade deal on a branded item normally selling to the trade at $20 per case.

Assume that the manufacturer normally averages sales to the trade of 5,000 cases per month—$100,000 at the normal trade price of $20 per case. If he cuts this price 10% to $18 for, say, a 30-day period, obviously he must sell through, *at the consumer level,* 11.1% more than this or a total of 5,556 cases merely to break even on a manufacturer's revenue basis.

Further assume that he operates on a 50% gross trading profit margin or $10 per case; the $2 per case trade discount must come out of the gross trading profit since it will still require $10 per case to pay for the cost of goods sold. Thus the G.T.P. on the deal goods is not $10 but $8, and the number of cases he must sell through at the consumer level to break even on a G.T.P. basis must be 6,250 cases—an increase of 25% for the 30-day period the deal is in effect and normal sales thereafter.

If the trade buyer decides to really take advantage of the deal, and many of them customarily act in this fashion even to the extent of buying only on deals when they know that the manufacturer has a consistent deal policy, he may buy ahead an additional month or two (at the expense of future purchases, of course), in which event sales to the consumer will have to increase 25% for each *extra* month of deal purchases as well. Consumer sales increases of this magnitude and duration are rarely possible on an established branded item, so one must conclude that most of these trade deals cost money and thus represent a cost chargeable against revenue rather than a promotion primarily designed to produce added sales at the consumer level.

This situation is becoming increasingly recognized by manufacturers, more and more of whom are now charging off the cost of trade deals and allowances against the top line and officially reporting sales as "gross sales less allowances."[2]

Ensuring Retailer Performance

While policing trade deals and following up on retailer performance are difficult, there are some guidelines manufacturers can follow:

- Tie the trade allowance to a cooperative advertising allowance requirement and demand proof of advertising. By tying the two together, the manufacturer is at least contractually entitled to determine whether or not the contract has been fulfilled.
- Require proof of the price reduction. This can take the form of tear sheets of advertising, shelf markers, or the like. Have the retailer send something to prove that the price was actually reduced as agreed.
- Set up a store monitoring system. This can be done through part-time help in various markets at a very reasonable cost. It also helps verify that the displays were built according to contract agreement on size, number, and location.
- Handle the verification elements of the trade alllowance through the advertising, sales promotion, or product manager, not through the sales force. When you turn the sales force into policemen, you weaken their sales effectiveness.

---

[2]Peckham, *The Wheel of Marketing*, p. 33.

There may be other ways to enforce retailer compliance with various trade promotion agreements, but we've found these usually work best.

Laws

While the general rule is that all trade promotions are legal as long as they are offered to all parties on an equitable basis, there are some specific legal regulations on trade allowances. The following general rules apply to almost all products and services:

- The Clayton Act forbids manufacturers from giving preferential price treatment to better or larger customers.
- The Robinson-Patman Act requires manufacturers to offer promotional aids to all their customers on a proportionately equal basis.
- Results of the Fred Meyer case define a manufacturer's customers as *not just* those who buy directly from the manufacturer (larger retailers). "Customers" are defined as including those who buy from wholesalers (smaller retailers). And they, too, must be treated equally.
- The Federal Trade Commission Guidelines suggest that promotional allowances to retailers must be spent on promotion. Of course, this creates problems for both sides.

Some Examples

While it is impossible to detail all the various types of trade allowances or trade deals, we illustrate three here as examples.

The Off-Invoice

Again, the most common type of trade allowance is the off-invoice. A typical example is illustrated in Figure 12-1.

The Free Goods Offer

The free goods offer is illustrated by the "Buy 12, get one free" offer from Duro-Lite shown in Figure 12-2.

The Performance Trade Allowance

There are literally hundreds of types of trade allowances that can be used as incentives to get the trade to either promote or support a sales promotion program at the retail level. For example, when Northern Tissue introduced its new package, it used a consumer sweepstakes. It also offered an off-label handling allowance of 25¢ per case to the retailer, plus a 50¢ per case, separate check, performance allowance. The performance agreement in this case required the retailer to promote the sweepstakes at the local level with an insert of a Northern ad mat in his local advertisement. To collect the 50¢

Sucaryl special deal*

from January 13, 1969 through February 28, 1969

ON ALL SUCARYL TABLETS— 12% OFF INVOICE

ITEM	REGULAR PRICE PER CASE	ALLOWANCE	DEAL PRICE PER CASE	DEAL PRICE PER BOTTLE
12/100 Tablets (Sodium)	$ 5.16	$ .62	$ 4.54	$ .378
12/100 Tablets (Calcium)	5.52	.66	4.86	.405
12/250 Tablets (Sodium)	11.16	1.34	9.82	.818
12/250 Tablets (Calcium)	11.88	1.43	10.45	.871
12/1000 Tablets (Sodium)	27.96	3.36	24.60	2.050
12/1000 Tablets (Calcium)	30.72	3.69	27.03	2.253
12/1½ oz Granular (Calcium)	7.80	.94	6.86	.572

SPECIAL ADDED BONUS—12% PLUS 6% OFF INVOICE ON LIQUID

ITEM	REGULAR PRICE PER CASE	ALLOWANCE	DEAL PRICE PER CASE	DEAL PRICE PER BOTTLE
12/6 oz Liquid (Sodium)	$ 7.08	$1.22	$ 5.86	$ .488
12/6 oz Liquid (Calcium)	7.08	1.22	5.86	.488
24/6 oz Liquid (Sodium)	14.04	2.43	11.61	.484
24/6 oz Liquid (Calcium)	14.04	2.43	11.61	.484
6/12 oz Liquid (Sodium)	6.78	1.17	5.61	.935
6/12 oz Liquid (Calcium)	6.78	1.17	5.61	.935
12/12 oz Liquid (Sodium)	13.44	2.33	11.11	.926
12/12 oz Liquid (Calcium)	13.44	2.33	11.11	.926
6/20 oz Liquid (Sodium)	10.74	1.86	8.88	1.480
6/20 oz Liquid (Sodium)	10.74	1.86	8.88	1.480
12/1 oz Concentrate Liquid (Calcium)	5.52	.95	4.57	.381

DISPLAY SIZE 77" high x 26" wide x 26" deep
CARTON SIZE 37" x 16" x 6½"
SHIPPING WT 15 lbs

FIGURE 12-1. Trade Allowance: Off-Invoice
Source: Courtesy of Sucaryl.

per case, the retailer had to provide Northern with proof of the use of the insert in the form of a tear-sheet from the newspaper.

When Helene Curtis needed to revitalize awareness of its "Every-night" brand of shampoo and conditioner, it developed a consumer promotion built around the idea of a free poster of John Travolta in the movie "Grease." To support this promotion with the trade, it offered a $2 per dozen off-invoice allowance on shampoo and a $2.87 per dozen off-invoice allowance on conditioner. In addition,

FIGURE 12-2. Trade Allowance: Free Goods
Source: Courtesy of Duro-lite Lamps, Inc.

Helene Curtis offered a 50¢ per dozen allowance for proof-of-performance. In this case, the performance could have been a price feature, an ad insert in the retail advertisement, or an in-store display. Whichever was used, the retailer had to supply proof that the promotion took place in the form of a photo, a tear-sheet, or a display card before the allowance was paid.

These are just two examples of the many types of performance allowances that can be used. The primary thing to remember is that the retailer must do something to earn the additional discount and must supply proof that the activity took place. Typically, performance takes the form of an in-store or advertising price feature, a feature in the store, an additional display, or a feature or illustration in the retailer's advertisement.

From this brief review of trade allowances and trade deals, our position should be clear: It's not a question of whether or not you should deal but of how effectively you deal in terms of increased sales and how efficient those deals are in terms of cost. Deals and allowances are here to stay. The goal of the sales promotion manager should be to (1) maximize their value to the brand and (2) control them and not let them control him. It's a tough job but it can be done.

Sampling

Sampling is the one sure method of putting a product directly into the consumer's hands. With most other sales promotion techniques, the consumer is required to take an extra step to actually get the product or the reward; i.e., take a coupon to the store, make a purchase to get a refund, and so on. Based on experience, sampling works well as a method of inducing trial of a product. It is particularly effective in introducing a new product.

In achieving trial or retrial of established products, however, sampling is not as efficient as couponing; i.e., it may be more successful in terms of generating trial but usually not on a cost-effective basis. However, the high trial rate and the extremely good conversion generated by sampling, which turns triers into buyers, usually makes it worthwhile.

As good as sampling is, however, it won't work for all products. Sampling is most successful when the product has a demonstrable point of difference or advantage over competition. That is, trying the product demonstrates that it is better, more effective, more efficient, etc. Sampling also works very well for products that can't really be explained in advertising, and need to be used or demonstrated for the benefit to be realized. Sampling doesn't work as well for products that are highly specialized or appeal to only small, very select markets, such as rug hookers, antique collectors, or others that are hard to identify by demographics or geographics. To be successfully sampled, the product should have mass appeal.

Sampling seems to work best for new products when it is preceded by four to six weeks of advertising. That generates interest, which the sample then converts into trial. There is one major caution with sampling, however. Never sample until there is sufficient distribution in retail stores to support the consumer interest built

Introduction

up by the sample. Nothing turns a consumer off more than to receive a product sample, try it, like it, want to buy it, and then not be able to find the product in the store.

The general objectives of a sampling program are to stimulate trial of a new or improved product, to encourage new use for an established product, or to call attention to a new package. Sampling can be used to build or broaden sales of an established product in fringe or new geographic areas. It can also be used to encourage trial by a new customer category or through a new distribution outlet.

Methods

Like couponing, sampling is distinguished by the distribution methods used to place the samples in the hands of prospects. As a general rule, the more direct the sampling plan, i.e., the more directly the product is put in the hands of the consumer, the more costly it is. Sampling distribution techniques are often limited or dictated by the product itself. If the product is bulky, a through-the-mail sampling plan is probably out. If it is perishable, in-packs or on-packs can't be used.

For most products there are eight major methods of sampling:

1. Direct Mail. The sample is sent directly to the prospect either through the Postal Service or through some other form of delivery, such as United Parcel Service. The major problem is the limitation on what can be mailed or shipped. New and pending postal restrictions are making sampling by mail somewhat difficult.

   In spite of the problems, experience has shown that direct mail is the best method of sampling and is 3 to 4 times more effective than couponing. Trial often reaches 70–80 percent of the homes sampled. The technique is very expensive, however, since the Postal Service charges by the ounce for handling the products.

2. Door-to-door. The product is personally delivered to the home, usually by an independent delivery or sampling service. The person making the delivery either leaves the sample on the doorstep or delivers it to the person answering the door. This is a very effective but again quite expensive method, probably the most expensive of all sampling techniques. It can be used only in urban areas, with high population density. In some communities, however, door-to-door sampling has been outlawed. It is also illegal to put the sampled product into any U.S. mailbox.

3. Central location/demonstrators. This is another method of putting the product directly into the prospect's hands. The

sample is given directly to prospects in a store, at a shopping mall, on a street corner, at a transportation terminal, or in some other public building, along with a sales message. This form of sampling is usually most effective if accompanied by a coupon or other incentive to purchase. If sampling is done in stores, it must be made available to all stores, as required by the Robinson-Patman Act.

4. Co-op or selective. Market-service groups have organized distribution methods to reach selective population subsamples, such as brides, the military, new mothers, and other groups, with a package of noncompetitive products that have special appeal to them. The cost is lower because of the co-op nature of the sampling procedure. For example, a sample package for brides is shipped to each new bride soon after she is married. The major advantage is the ability to reach groups that might otherwise be difficult (and therefore expensive) to sample.

5. Media. Some products can be sampled through the media, most notably newspapers and magazines. If the product is small and thin enough, it can be either bound in or inserted in the publication and sampled with the publication's circulation. The major advantage is the home delivery of the sample and the opportunity to deliver a sales message at the same time. This sampling method, however, can be expensive, because of the necessary production costs. Media sampling is not considered a very effective technique since only about 1 percent of media circulation tries the product after receiving the sample.

6. Sample pack in stores. An increasingly important method of sampling is the sale of a trial size package in the retail stores. Miniatures of the product are manufactured and sold to the retailer. The retailer then sells the samples directly to the consumer, usually with a margin higher than that of competitive products. This is an effective way to get trial at a very low cost. In some instances there may even be a small profit to the manufacturer. Retailers like this sampling method because it gives them margin on a product that was formerly given away free.

7. Free sample with coupon. A free sample of the actual product is given away with a coupon. The consumer gets the sample at the retail store through a mailed or media-distributed coupon that is redeemed by the retailer. Another method is for the consumer to mail a coupon to the manufacturer and receive a free sample through the mail. This approach has been very effective for many products because it reaches

only those with interest in the product. It is expensive since the manufacturer must pay either the handling fee of the retailer or the postage to return the product through the mail.

8. In-pack or on-pack. A noncompeting product may carry the sampling offer or the sample to the consumer. In this method a free sample of the product is used as a premium by the product carrying the sample. In most cases, there is very limited exposure or trial through this technique since the sample is limited to present users of the carrying product. This method has the lowest trial rate of all sampling procedures, but it is also the least expensive.

There are, of course, other methods of distributing samples of a product, but these are the most widely used.

The Advantages

As we said in the beginning, sampling is the most effective way yet devised of gaining trial of a product. There are, additionally, these specific advantages.

1. Sampling is flexible and can be quite selective. Depending on the needs of the manufacturer, a sampling program can be designed to fit specific program requirements for most products. The sampling program can be made broad scale and massive, if necessary. Some products, such as Gillette's Atra razor and S. C. Johnson's Agree shampoo, distributed millions of samples in their introductions. Indeed, the entire country can be covered in a short period of time, if desired.

2. Sampling usually provides fairly fast delivery, which results in immediate action at the retail stores. Unlike advertising, which often requires several exposures to the message to get action, sampling puts the product in the hands of the prospect and gains immediate trial. The consumer then responds fairly quickly to the product.

3. Sampling can be low in cost in relation to the amount of trial produced. Some forms of sampling can provide a sample to the prospect at a very low cost, although usually not quite as efficiently as a couponing program.

4. Sampling is sometimes the only way to convert some people to the product. Where there is high brand loyalty, sampling may be the only method of encouraging consumers to consider the new brand.

5. The trade recognizes the value of sampling. Since sampling results in rather quick action at the retail level, retailers are usually willing to stock a brand with a sound sampling program.

6. With a sampling program, the trade can often be encouraged to develop displays or features to go with it. This off-shelf feature activity helps build and expand sales for the product.

7. Sampling can often be used to build distribution for an established brand. It is a particularly effective method of getting additional distribution in areas where the brand is not well represented or in fringe areas of distribution.

Sampling plans also have these disadvantages.

The Disadvantages

1. Sampling is a very expensive sales promotion device. While high trial can be generated, it is often at a very high cost. The manufacturer must determine whether he can afford the cost of sampling since the cost of the product, the distribution method, and the accompanying promotional materials can add up quickly.

2. Sampling only works for products with high volume and broad-based appeal. For more specialized products, sampling may lack precision because it is often difficult to obtain a distribution list for highly segmented or highly selective groups of consumers.

3. Sampling, on a dollar for dollar basis, is often less cost-efficient than other forms of sales promotion, particularly couponing, even though couponing does not achieve the same trial rate as sampling.

4. There often is a lack of control over the delivery of the samples. While the Postal Service has increased its rates dramatically, there has been no resulting improvement in delivery time or condition. The manufacturer is simply at the mercy of the delivery organization as to whether the sample arrives intact or on time.

5. A sampling plan always faces problems with theft or pilferage, regardless of the method used or the value of the product. Theft can occur anywhere along the distribution line, from the delivery service to store employees.

Sampling has other disadvantages but these seem to be the major ones. While they are troublesome, most can be overcome with a sound, well-planned program.

On the following pages, we have listed a number of suggestions and ideas that may be helpful to you in planning your own sampling program. However, the most effective way to develop a sampling program is to work with one of the several excellent market-service organizations that provide this service. You'll find a list of some of these groups in Appendix II.

Some Guidelines

Costs

It is impossible to give accurate costs of sampling programs, simply because they vary so widely and change so rapidly, but we have illustrated several methods to give you an idea of approximate costs:

1. The cost of direct mail depends on the weight of the product and the postal charges at the time. The cost per ounce to mail a sample weighing 3 ounces in 1980 was 8.75¢. In addition to the cost of the sample, you must include the charges for the mailing list, the carton, the addressing, the handling, the postage, and any return materials, such as a coupon.

2. Door-to-door distribution costs vary widely, depending on the number of homes to be covered, how close the homes are together, the availability of a sampling organization in the community, the location of the city, etc. For example, in Chicago and suburbs the cost of hand-delivering a sample to homes in 1980 was approximately $150 per thousand. This cost is based on the advertiser furnishing a 3- to 4-ounce sample and the distribution company inserting the sample in a clear poly bag and hanging the sample on the doors of homes. A coupon can be included for the same cost. It is estimated that each person in the delivery crew can cover about 225 homes per day in fairly compact neighborhoods. (A note of caution: Some communities have outlawed door-to-door sampling. Find out if you are allowed to sample in the community before making your plans.) Again, include the cost of the product, the door-hanger or other method of attaching to the door, coupons, etc.

3. Usually a flat rate per day is charged for a product distributor/demonstrator of the product, regardless of how many units are distributed. In Chicago in 1980, cost per day for a demonstrator was approximately $125 minimum, plus transportation and cost of product. Don't forget to include the cost of the product, any sales promotion materials, and any coupons that might also be distributed.

4. A cooperative mailing to specialized groups is normally less expensive than many other forms of sampling. For example, you may participate in a co-op sampling program such as Donnelley's Carol Wright mailing. As with the other sampling programs, be sure to include the cost of the product and any sales promotion material, in addition to the actual cost of the co-op program.

5. The in-pack or on-pack method usually costs less than any other type of sampling. Since the only costs are usually for the product, the attachment or insertion, and any promotional

material, the sample can get to the consumer with little or no actual distribution cost.

As a general rule, the following costs can be incurred in the preparation or execution of a sampling program. Use this as a check list.

- The sampled product
- Direct mail or list charges
- Postage or distribution costs
- Handling fees, such as those charged by a direct mail organization
- Advertising or other sales promotion material costs that might be included in the sample package
- The cost of cartons, boxes, or other materials to distribute the product
- Retailer and/or clearing house charges for coupons distributed with the sample, including the face value of the coupon
- Cost of insertion or attachment, for in- or on-pack sampling

Product Selection

Some products simply sample better than others do. Generally, products that are new or improved make the best samples. Products with a demonstrable difference over competition are also effective samples. Usually products that are frequently purchased and have a high number of potential users also do very well.

Products that do not normally do well in a sampling program are those that have a slow turnover or are not purchased very frequently. Also, products that require a personal selection or those in which there is a wide variety of choices in such things as colors, odors, and flavors do not sample effectively. This would include such products as after-shave lotion, fingernail polish, and lipstick.

Other products that do not do well in sampling programs are those without an obvious consumer benefit or those not noticeably different from competition. As a general rule, mature or established brands do not benefit very much from sampling, unless it is done in a new area or a fringe territory.

Timing

Usually sampling works best if done just before any seasonal upswing in sales or use of the product. This helps to generate usage and can result in extra sales.

A cardinal rule of sampling is not to sample until there is sufficient retail distribution in the market to support the sample. Normally, this means at least 50 percent distribution in retail stores that normally stock the product. You can't benefit from a sampling program if the prospects can't buy at retail, and consumers get angry if they can't buy after trying the sample.

Be cautious of sampling a product with a low inventory or a very high turnover at retail. A successful sampling program can often create out-of-stock conditions in the retail store. Pretest the sample first to see the results before going all-out with this type of program.

Size

While there is no hard and fast rule, the sample should always be large enough for the consumer to get a fair trial of the product. Of course, that depends on what benefit you are claiming for the product. If it is something that tastes good, one serving can be enough. If it is something that requires continued use to see the benefits, then a larger sample is in order. As a general rule, a regular size produces more trial than smaller samples. If you do decide to go with a smaller size, make it a miniature of the larger package. That way, customers know what the product looks like when they go to the store to buy it after the trial.

Trial and Usage

As a comparison of what couponing and sampling can achieve in terms of triers becoming users, Charles Frederick, Jr., of Ogilvy & Mather, Inc., suggests that the conversion rate, that is, the percentage of triers who become users, is always lower for sampling than for couponing. It is usually 20–30 percent for sampling but 30–40 percent for couponing. Based on his experience, Frederick says the relation between trial and usage for 100 homes sampled and couponed usually looks like this:[1]

As you can see, while sampling does better than couponing at obtaining trial, it does worse than couponing in converting triers into users. Thus, it is technically less efficient.

	Sample	Mail Coupon
Total homes	100	100
Trial	80	20
Usage	20	7
Rate of conversion	25%	35%

The One Major Rule in Media

If you are offering a sample through a media advertisement, don't bury the offer in the copy. Make it bold and clear. Say, *Here is a*

---

[1]Charles Frederick, Jr., "What Ogilvy & Mather Has Learned About Sales Promotion," a speech given to the Association of National Advertisers, September 1973.

sample. Send for it now. Don't make it hard to find or hard to read. The idea is to get the product in the hands of the prospect, not win an art award.

On the following pages, we illustrate some examples of sound sampling methods. While there are other ways to accomplish the same goal, we believe these are the most effective.

Some Examples

Direct Mail Sampling

General Mills sampled its new cereal, Crispy Wheats 'n Raisins, through direct mail. It's shown in Figure 13-1. A 1.5-ounce package, including a 7¢ coupon, was mailed to individual addresses on the list. Since the sample was a miniature of the actual product package, the consumer knew what to look for in the store.

In some select cases, samples are mailed directly to individuals and street addresses. This is effective but very expensive. An alternative to mailing to an individual is simply to mail a sample to every home on a postal route. That is what Beecham Products did with the sampling program for its new Aqua-Fresh toothpaste. A mailing carton with the product, containing an information folder, was sent to all homes on selected postal routes throughout the country.

Door-to-Door Sampling

Although one of the most expensive of all forms of sampling, the delivery of a sample directly to the door of a prospective customer is often worth the expense. It is one sure way to get the product into the hands of the consumer and, in some cases, the only way.

While door-to-door sampling was once a thriving business, it is now used much less frequently. Urban sprawl and the greater spacing of houses, the increased cost of labor and delivery, and the increasing number of working wives have turned door-to-door sampling into a rather special device. In spite of these changes, however, door-to-door sampling is still a vital ingredient in the promotion mix of many new products and in the revitalization of older ones.

One of the biggest advantages of door-to-door delivery is the opportunity to get a sample of a product that is difficult to deliver in any other form directly to the home of a consumer. For example, when Thomas' English muffins began distributing its product in Chicago, it used a four-pack of the product in a poly bag that was hung on the door of homes. This way, Thomas was able to deliver a perishable product directly and to control the product's handling until it was placed on the prospect's door. To further strengthen the sampling program, Thomas included a 15¢ coupon in the bag for use on the next purchase. (Figure 13-2.)

FIGURE 13-1. Sample: Direct Mail
Source: Reproduced with the permission of General Mills, Inc.

Central Location/Demonstration

There are many forms of central location sampling. In the most common, a person stands on a street corner or in a public place and simply gives away samples of the product. This method is often used by cigarette and candy companies to demonstrate a new brand or a new product. An alternative to this, which makes the delivery of the product a bit more selective, is a near-store sampling program. In this case, people are stationed near a store or in a shopping center and give samples of the product to interested consumers.

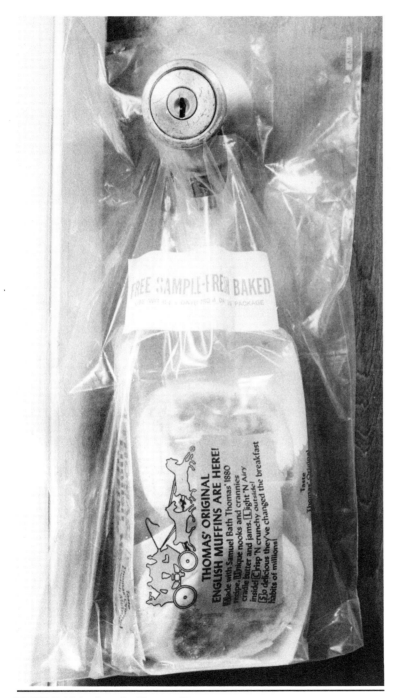

FIGURE 13-2. Sample: Door-to-Door
Source: Courtesy of Thomas' English Muffins.

Figure 13-3 illustrates a near-store sampling program for Mainstay Dog Food, part of a national sampling program conducted by Stratmar Systems, Inc., for Ralston Purina. More than 4,500,000 two-pound samples were distributed in this new-product introduction.

FIGURE 13-3. Sample: Central Location/Demonstration
Source: Courtesy of Stratmar Systems, Inc.

The cost of this kind of sampling can vary widely. The estimated cost for central location sampling in Chicago in 1981 was approximately $40 per thousand, plus the cost of the product being sampled. Most street distributors can distribute up to 3,000 samples per day, depending on street traffic and the type of product. While central location sampling is usually quoted on a cost-per-thousand basis, retail store demonstrators normally are figured on a per diem basis to include time and service, plus transportation. The cost of the product being demonstrated is additional.

Cooperative Mailing

In a cooperative mailing, several companies go together to send samples in a common package. Figure 13-4 shows a co-op mailing featuring Agree creme rinse and conditioner from S. C. Johnson & Son. Included in the package was a sample of Kotex Lightdays PantiLiners from Kimberly-Clark. Johnson also added a coupon from Edge shaving gel, another one of its products. Thus, the cost of the sample was split by the three brands involved.

FIGURE 13-4. Sample: Co-op Mailing
Source: Courtesy of S.C. Johnson & Son.

In-Pack or On-Pack

Alka Seltzer Plus wanted to sample its cold remedy. While its budget was large enough to cover the cost of the sample, it wasn't large enough to cover distribution. Through a third party, Cross-Ruff Clearing House, Bic was selected as the sample carrier. Samples of Alka Seltzer Plus were packed into 5 million Bic shaver packages (Figure 13-5). This got the sample into the home and into the bathroom where cold remedies are usually found. It provided a strong promotional push for Bic and an excellent sampling device for Alka Seltzer Plus.

FIGURE 13-5. Sample: On-pack Cross-Ruff
Source: A Cross Ruff Clearing House Promotion.

Media Sample

An example of a media sample is illustrated in Figure 13-6. Samples of Ziploc heavy-duty freezer bags, along with a coupon for a cents-off purchase, were included in a packet that was inserted as an advertising supplement in several Midwest newspapers. The samples were therefore distributed to all newspaper subscribers on the media list on that particular day.

FIGURE 13-6. Sample: Media Distributed

Source: Courtesy of Dow Chemical Co. Ziploc is a trademark of Dow
Chemical Co.

Sample Package

New, improved Clorox 2 was sampled through trial packages sold
in retail stores, as illustrated in Figure 13-7. The package was a
miniature of the regular Clorox 2 package and contained enough
product for one use. It was prepriced at 15¢.

Free Sample with Coupon

Often, the most effective method of distribution is simply to give
the product away at the retail store. That's what Quaker Oats did
for its Aunt Jemima buttermilk pancake mix. Directions: Simply
cut the coupon from the newspaper and take it to your favorite food
store to receive the 3¼-pound sample. (See Figure 13-8.) It's an

FIGURE 13-7. Sample: Package
Source: By permission of The Clorox Company.

expensive method of sampling but one that really gets action. One caution: Have the product in the stores with widespread distribution before you schedule this type of sampling plan.

From these examples, you can see that sampling is often the most expensive promotion vehicle available to the sales promotion manager. It is, however, an excellent device that can operate independently of a busy sales force to stimulate trial of a new or improved product, build sales volume immediately, and force distribution.

FIGURE 13-8. Sample: Free with Coupon

Source: William A. Robinson, *Best Sales Promotions of 1977/78* (Chicago: Crain Books, 1979), p. 138.

Point-of-Purchase Materials

Usually, when one mentions sales promotion, the first image that comes to mind is that of a supermarket or drugstore festooned with banners, posters, signs, and displays filling the windows and aisles and covering the walls and ceiling. While these items are correctly labeled as sales promotion materials, they are usually better described as point-of-purchase materials. P-o-p's, as they are often called, are those items which are used in and around the retail store to call special attention to products or services, particularly to those the retailer wants to promote, such as special bargains, features, or reduced prices. P-o-p's are often used simply to reinforce the advertising message received by the consumer through the media. With more than 10,000 items available in the average supermarket and nearly 15,000 in the average drug store, p-o-p's are a vital link in both the retailer's and manufacturer's efforts to promote the product to consumers who are ready to buy right at the point-of-purchase.

In this chapter, we will take a brief look at point-of-purchase materials, particularly those used with consumer products. Obviously, p-o-p materials will vary widely since their use is based on the nature of the product and the retail store in which it is sold. There are, however, some general guidelines for the planning and development of sound, effective p-o-p materials. For more information, you may wish to contact the Point-of-Purchase Advertising Institute in New York City. As the official organization for p-o-p's, they have a wealth of information on the subject.

In the past twenty or so years, point-of-purchase materials have become increasingly important in the sale of most types of consumer products in retail stores. As self-service retailing has expanded from the food and drug stores to hardware, general merchandise,

Introduction

and discount stores, much more emphasis has been put on p-o-p materials to provide the shopper with information and pricing on the products on display. In many instances, p-o-p materials are used to guide the shopper to various sections of the store or to cross-merchandise products. Often, the p-o-p materials provide the shopper with the only additional information he or she may receive about a product prior to making a final purchase decision in a self-service outlet. Further, p-o-p materials are used to help influence the shopper to make the increasingly important impulse purchase. They are also used to remind shoppers of items they may have left off their shopping list.

For some years many retailers discounted the use of p-o-p materials in the store. They believed that p-o-p's contributed to a cluttered look and that signs, posters, and other materials detracted from the appearance of the store. Fortunately, many retailers are rediscovering the advantages that point-of-purchase materials can provide. There seems to be a resurgence of interest in making the retail outlet an interesting and exciting place to be. That atmosphere is heightened with effective p-o-p materials.

Types   Point-of-purchase materials come in many shapes, sizes, and types. Perhaps the easiest method of distinguishing among them is simply to differentiate between those prepared by the retailer himself for use in his store and those provided by the manufacturer or the marketer of a product. Those prepared by the retailer may range from a scrawled sign in the window, announcing a close-out on a product, to very complete and distinctive materials used to promote a store-wide event. For example, for the "British Fortnight" promotion developed by Neiman-Marcus, most of the materials used in the stores were prepared by the company's sales promotion department. Figure 14-1 illustrates the lengths to which Neiman-Marcus goes to provide a shopping atmosphere through the use of p-o-p materials.

Manufacturers or marketers also furnish a great deal of the p-o-p materials found in many retail outlets. For example, Figure 14-2 illustrates just some of the in-store display items that Seagram and Ocean Spray developed for use at retail to help promote "The Firecracker," a drink combining Seagram whiskey and Ocean Spray cranberry juice cocktail.

In this chapter, we will deal only with manufacturer-originated p-o-p materials, i.e., materials developed by the manufacturer or the marketer and furnished to the retailer to help promote the sale of a specific brand of product or to influence the retailer to feature a line of products offered by the manufacturer. Within this category, there are three basic types of p-o-p materials:

FIGURE 14-1. Neiman-Marcus "British Fortnight" Promotion
Source: Courtesy of Neiman-Marcus.

Signage

Signage is often considered a form of p-o-p although it may technically not be. Signage includes all those items of a permanent nature,
usually on the outside of the retail outlet, used to help identify the
retailer either as a member of a specific group of stores or outlets or

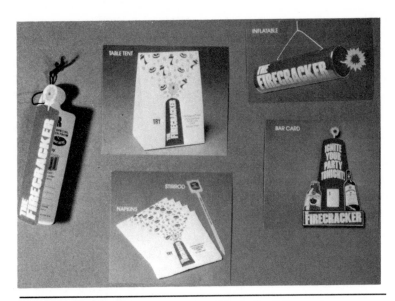

FIGURE 14-2. Seagram-Ocean Spray "Firecracker" Promotion
Source: William A. Robinson, *100 Best Sales Promotions of 1976/77*
(Chicago: Crain Books, 1977), p. 15.

as a retail outlet for a specific brand of product. For example, the signs around and on a Texaco service station not only identify the outlet as a service station for automobiles but also help promote the Texaco brand name. Manufacturers sometimes furnish signage to retailers to help identify the outlet as one in which specific brands of products are available. Figure 14-3 shows some of the various types of retail signage that Borden offers its dairy products retailers.

Branded P-o-p Materials

These are in-store p-o-p's on which the manufacturer's brand is prominently featured, includng posters, signs, and displays of all kinds. The material may be used to promote a special offer, a sales promotion event, or simply to reinforce the media sales message.

Non-Branded P-o-p Materials

In some situations, manufacturers or marketers provide retailers with display or point-of-purchase materials that contain no brand name and promote only a generic sales idea. The American Dairy Association has done this for many years with its June Dairy Month promotion. The American Dairy Association also has developed p-o-p materials that emphasize only the sale of dairy products, such as milk, cheese, butter, and yogurt, rather than some specific

REAR PANEL

SIDE PANEL

LOGO

FIGURE 14-3. Signage: Borden, Inc.
Source: Courtesy of Borden, Inc.

brand. Figure 14-4 illustrates some of this non-branded American Dairy Association material.

Some manufacturers may also offer the retailer very general decorative materials that contain no brand identification at all and may not even mention a product or an event. These materials are used only to help make the store more attractive and are used primarily to develop a better working relationship between the manufacturer and the retail store operator.

Permanent vs. Temporary P-o-p Materials

In addition to the above classifications, point-of-purchase materials are also separated on the basis of whether they are permanent or temporary. Usually signage is considered permanent, while such things as paper banners are temporary since they are usually designed for use for a very short time. In Figure 14-5 you will find examples of two award-winning permanent p-o-p displays that manufacturers have offered retailers recently. Note that each of them provided a method of calling attention to the product and distinguishing it from competition in the retail outlet.

FIGURE 14-4. Non-Branded P-o-p Materials: American Dairy Association

Source: William A. Robinson, *Best Sales Promotions of 1977/78* (Chicago: Crain Books, 1979), p. 30.

An example of temporary p-o-p materials is shown in Figure 14-6, a shelf-talker with a cash refund offer form for L'Oréal shampoo and hair color. This is considered a temporary piece because once the refund coupons are removed, the material has served its purpose and will be removed.

The Advantages

Point-of-purchase materials offer several advantages to the marketer, retailer, and consumer. Each is discussed on the following pages.

Advantages to the Consumer

P-o-p materials give the consumer more information on products or services available in the retail store. In many instances, the materials enable the consumer to compare various brands in order to make the wisest selection. With the reduction in the number of clerks in most retail stores, p-o-p materials are almost required in many outlets. In addition to furnishing information, point-of-pur-

FIGURE 14-5. Permanent P-o-p Materials: Realemon
Source: Courtesy of the Point-of-Purchase Advertising Institute, Inc.

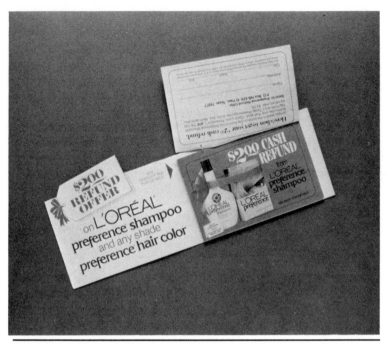

FIGURE 14-6. Temporary P-o-p Materials: L'Oréal Hair Products
Source: Robinson, *100 Best Sales Promotions of 1976/7*, p. 38.

chase materials also provide a reminder for or call attention to products that the consumer might not have thought of or might have forgotten.

Advantages to the Retailer

Generally, the greatest advantage of manufacturer-originated point-of-purchase materials is that the retailer has better-constructed, more complete, and more attractive display materials on products in his store than he could provide himself. Since the manufacturer produces the material in quantity, it is usually available to the retailer at little or no cost. Furthermore, good p-o-p materials help bring the media advertising message right into the retail store to help reinforce and complete the sale. Finally, p-o-p materials help encourage the all-important impulse sale. Studies have shown that as many as 30 percent of the items purchased in food stores were not on the shopping list made prior to the store visit. These impulse sales are vital to the success of most retail stores.

Advantages to the Manufacturer

For many marketers, point-of-purchase materials in the retail store are the most vital link in the selling chain for the product. Since many manufacturers' media advertising is necessarily limited by high media costs, the advertising messages about the product must be reinforced at the retail level. P-o-p materials provide that link. Thus, a dramatic media advertising campaign that the consumer has seen or heard is featured again, just at the point-of-purchase. This synergism often helps complete the sale. In addition, p-o-p's are the last message a consumer usually has before the purchase. Decisions can often be switched through strong, effective p-o-p materials. Finally, point-of-purchase is usually the least expensive advertising medium for the manufacturer. Since the primary cost is in the development of the material, the cost-per-impression, spread among many retailers, is usually quite low.

While it might appear that p-o-p materials are the ideal advertising medium, there are some disadvantages to the consumer, the retailer, and the manufacturer.

The Disadvantages

Disadvantages to the Consumer

The only real disadvantage of point-of-purchase materials to the consumer occurs if they are overdone in the store. No one likes to shop in a jungle, and when p-o-p materials are used to excess the consumer finds products and information more difficult to obtain.

Disadvantages to the Retailer

The primary complaint of the retailer about point-of-purchase materials furnished by the manufacturer is that he simply can't use all that is available. All products in a store can't be featured at one time. Picking and choosing among all the available materials can be a time-consuming and costly method of planning retail store displays. Further, in some cases, in their enthusiasm to provide dominant materials, manufacturers forget the needs of the retailer. Thus, the displays are too large, the materials too gaudy, or the ideas not practical. Because of this, the retailer may find that while much material is available to him, a great deal of it is not truly usable in his store.

Disadvantages to the Manufacturer

Directly related to the concerns of the retailer are those of the manufacturer or supplier of the point-of-purchase materials. If the materials are produced and shipped to the retailer and then not used, the money invested is simply wasted. Material that might help produce sales for both the retailer and the manufacturer never sees the light of day in the store and is finally discarded. In these cases, no matter how low the individual unit cost, the manufacturer has simply wasted part of his sales promotion budget. This is by far the greatest problem for the manufacturer. Another disadvantage often cited is that the material may not reach the right consumer; i.e., the most ineffective retail stores use the material while those with the greatest potential do not. Thus, there is waste even though the material is used and displayed in the retail outlets.

Some Guidelines

The key ingredient in the successful use of point-of-purchase materials is in the planning and production stages. The Point-of-Purchase Advertising Institute, based on the experience of its members, has developed a very complete description of considerations in this area of sales promotion, which follows:

Planning and Development

When the advertiser's marketing plan includes the utilization of point-of-purchase merchandising materials, he may elect to assign the development of a display or a merchandising program to a point-of-purchase producer.

Some producers have staff and facilities to plan, design, develop, produce and distribute. Some specialize in planning and development, but contract with other facilities for production and distribution. Some also use external design sources. In some cases the advertiser does the planning and development and contracts only for production and distribution.

Because of the differences in producer activities, and in the desires of various advertisers, it is most important that both parties are fully aware of just what each other's contribution will be before undertaking a particular project.

Planning Is a Cooperative Effort

In the great majority of instances, planning and development of point-of-purchase materials take place with the producer and the advertiser working together. Few advertisers find it economical to maintain a staff with the variety of skills necessary for the creation of their programs. The most efficient planning takes place when the advertiser and the producer work as a team. For this reason, the point-of-purchase producer should be consulted in the initial stage of the planning of the materials for the campaign.

The Role of Advertiser

The advertiser usually delegates the point-of-purchase planning phase to specialists within his company. These specialists may be sales promotion managers, merchandising managers, brand managers, or merchandising departments functioning with responsibility for planning and development. They are guided by designated budgets in evaluating the development of displays and programs which meet their objectives.

The Role of the Producer

In the planning stage the producer, through his sales representatives and his creative department, counsels the advertiser on such matters as size, form, and function of point-of-purchase merchandising materials. To do this the producer should have a working knowledge of marketing, customs, laws and special limitation in particular fields of distribution, and the basic materials available to him.

The producer's assignment may include all or part of the actual design and appearance of the unit, the basic idea, concept, illustration, suggested copy, detailed layout of elements, engineering and structural features.

The presentation takes the form agreed upon with the advertiser and may include sketches, constructions and/or models for consideration.

Information Needed for Effective Planning

It is recommended that producer and advertiser reach preliminary joint agreement for the most efficient handling of project specifications. Past experience has shown that the best projects have resulted when both producer and advertiser have a comprehensive understanding of all elements of the project. Producers and advertisers are encouraged to develop preliminary checklists to aid employees in the successful accomplishment of projects. Listed here are samples of considerations that you may wish to include in such a checklist:

What is the advertiser's marketing objective for the product or service?

What is the advertiser's point-of-purchase objective for the product or service?

What is the specific purpose of the proposed unit or campaign?

What is the theme of the total advertising program, and, if it differs, of the point-of-purchase program?

Is the point-of-purchase to be coordinated with the total advertising program?

What advertiser personnel are involved with this project?

What advertising message will the particular unit carry?

What must the unit do in addition to presenting its advertising message at the point-of-purchase?

How and where will the point-of-purchase materials be used?

How long will they be used?

What types of point-of-purchase materials have been used by the advertiser in the past?

What types are currently being used?

How have these units been accepted by the advertiser's sales force, by wholesalers, retailers and consumers?

What has been their effect on sales?

What is the competition using?

In what types of retail outlets will the materials be used?

Is product available?

What is the budget for the program?

What are the terms of payment?

Who has purchase order responsibility?

What quantities are required?

What is the project timetable: design-approval-production-distribution?

How will they be packed, shipped, distributed and installed?

What legal restrictions must be taken into consideration?

Who will own the design? Client? Producer?

Are developmental costs speculative? Billed separately or included in the production price?

What policies and procedures govern the submission and approval of bids?

The Creative Function

When the creative function is assigned, the producer's responsibility may include illustration, copy, detailed layout, engineering and structural features as required. It is, therefore, necessary for both the advertiser and the producer to understand the following in advance:

Cost of Creativity

To provide the necessary creative services, the producer incurs a variety of expenses. These may include maintenance of a design and engineering staff, space, and other facilities. To maintain a design and engineering staff which is available when, and to the extent, the advertiser needs it, requires substantial annual investment. The advertiser expects to pay for the use of the producer's talents and facilities. Compensation to the producer may be separate, or the cost may be included in the unit price paid for the materials.

Some advertisers reimburse those producers who have worked on the project in the creative stages, but who do not get the order. Many advertisers prefer to pay for these services as they are used.

Since every program has budget limitations, it is to the mutual advantage of both producer and advertiser to come to a clear understanding of such cost before work begins.

Presentation of Sketches and Models

The producer normally executes sketches in black and white or color (in some cases blank models) because there is no other way for him to show how he proposes to solve a particular merchandising problem. Such presentation sketches represent a preliminary study of the advertiser's merchandising problem by the producer. It may be necessary to prepare a complete mechanical design in order to make sure the unit is practical, and to insure a realistic price quotation. The rough sketch itself may represent only a fraction of the expense incurred in preparing the presentation.

The advertiser should be clear in his assignment. He may ask for sketches only. The producer should not proceed with mechanical designs or comps until this work is approved by the advertiser. This procedure will reduce expenses at the outset.

For the experienced advertiser, rough sketches are usually sufficient to be able to approve further development or to suggest a new approach. The ability to do this saves the advertiser and the producer substantial sums of money. Further necessary development should be agreed upon before proceeding.

Generally, the creative producer is not interested in developing sketches or models for profit. The conduct of his business as a producer of point-of-purchase merchandising materials and services is the source of profit.

Summary

Good point-of-purchase programs result from proper planning and development. Good planning and development comes only through the proper function of all the roles and responsibilities discussed in this section.[1]

---

[1]*The Buyer's Guide* (New York: The Point-of-Purchase Advertising Institute, 1979).

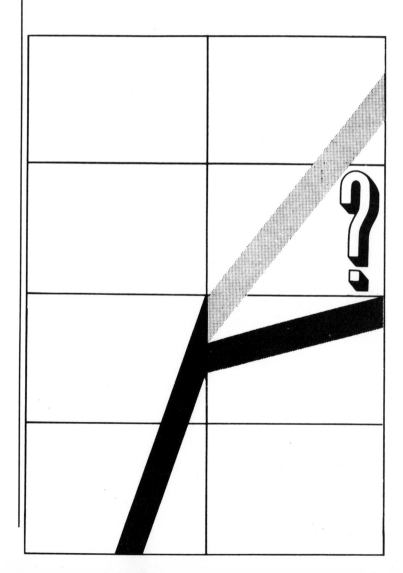

Some Final Thoughts on Sales Promotion

On the preceding pages, we've attempted to give you a concise view of sales promotion and sales promotion techniques. In a field this dynamic, new developments have already appeared on the scene while this book was in press. That's to be expected, and it's also what makes the field of sales promotion so much fun. It's always different, exciting, and open to a new idea.

There are probably some areas in which you need more information or material. Certainly, you'll need more specifics before you plan a major program. If so, contact your sales promotion agency and suppliers. They are the ones who can and will provide you with the information you will need to make your program a success.

As we have stressed throughout this book, planning and execution are the two mainsprings of a successful sales promotion program. Eugene Mahany, in a speech to the Association of National Advertisers Annual Meeting in 1977, quoted the "Ten Promotion Commandments," which are used at Dancer-Fitzgerald-Sample, a major advertising agency. We think they provide a sound finale to this book.

    I. Thou shall not plan promotion without first specifying objective and budget.
    II. Thou shall select only the right promotion techniques to attain specific objectives.
    III. Thou shall direct thy promotions to thy target audience.
    IV. Thou shall not use confusing, complicated consumer copy.
    V. Thou shall not be greedy in consumer purchase requirements.

VI. Thou shall support promotion with advertising when merited.

VII. Thou shall test any major program in which there is no brand experience.

VIII. Thou shall not wait 'til the last minute to plan.

IX. Thou shall always honor the "KISS" philosophy.*

X. Thou shall always consult with promotion specialists when planning promotions.

*Keep It Simple, Stupid.[1]

If you follow these sales promotion "commandments" you should be well on your way to success.

---

[1] Eugene Mahany, "Improving Payouts of Consumer Promotions," a speech given to the Association of National Advertisers, Hot Springs, Virginia, October 1977.

European Sales Promotion

Since sales promotion is used so widely in the United States, we naturally assume that the same is true in other countries. Unfortunately, that is not always the case. For example, the marketer in Europe faces dramatic differences in what can and cannot be done to promote his products. In many cases, there are legal restrictions and unwritten laws developed by the government. In other instances, there are cultural differences that preclude the use of various sales promotion tools we take as common and ordinary.

One of the greatest problems, particularly in Europe, is the consumer dislike and distrust of all forms of advertising and promotion. In part, this is due to the newness of advertising and marketing techniques, most of which have been introduced abroad only since the close of World War II. When these marketing techniques clash with tradition, tradition usually wins. As a result, many marketing activities are considered to be in bad taste or otherwise unacceptable. This seems particularly true on the Continent and in countries where mass marketing and mass merchandising are only now beginning to mature as retailing forms.

In addition to the cultural differences and lack of acceptance, most European countries have placed rather severe restrictions on the types and methods of sales promotion that can be used. The International Advertising Association has made a detailed study of what sales promotion and marketing techniques can and can't be used in each country. If you market internationally, you'll want a copy of their report, which is available through their offices in New York City. For our purposes, though, a brief look at the restrictions in Europe will be enlightening. It should be noted that these regulations, like many others, are subject to change. If you are seriously interested in sales promotion in a European country, we suggest you contact the proper officials in that country to make sure that your plan is not only legal but acceptable as well. As a general guide, however, you will find the chart in Table A-1, prepared by Benton & Bowles, helpful. It shows the general acceptability of 46 separate sales promotion techniques in European countries, including those directed at the trade as well as the consumer.

Please note the keys to the chart:

Y indicates that this technique is *generally* legal (although often restricted) and fairly regularly used.

P indicates that this technique is basically legal, but has never

PROMOTION EVENT 1. Consumer Oriented A. SPECIAL FACTORY PACKS	Belgium	Denmark	France	Germany	Italy	Netherlands	Norway	Spain	Sweden	U.K.
1. Price Pack	Y	Y	Y	Y	Y	Y	Y	Y	Y	Y
2. Premium Pack	N	N	N	P	Y	Y	N	Y	Y	Y
3. Reusable Container Pack	Y	Y	P	P	Y	Y	Y	Y	P	Y
4. Coupon Packs	Y	N	Y	N	Y	Y	N	Y	N	Y
5. Bonus Product Pack	Y	Y	Y	N	Y	Y	Y	Y	Y	Y
6. Multiple Unit Pack	Y	Y	Y	P	Y	Y	Y	Y	Y	Y
7. Trial-Size Pack	Y	P	Y	Y	Y	Y	Y	Y	Y	Y
B. COUPONING										
8. Mailed	Y	Y	Y	P	Y	Y	N	Y	Y	Y
9. Media Delivered	Y	Y	Y	P	P	Y	N	Y	P	Y
10. Cross-Ruff	N	N	N	P	Y	Y	N	P	P	Y
11. Delayed Mail	Y	P	Y	N	P	Y	N	P	P	Y
12. Dealer Coupons	Y	P	Y	P	P	Y	N	P	P	Y
C. SAMPLING										
13. Home Delivery	Y	Y	Y	Y	Y	Y	Y	Y	P	Y
14. Cross-Ruff	Y	N	Y	Y	Y	Y	N	Y	P	Y
15. Mail-In	Y	P	Y	Y	P	Y	Y	Y	Y	Y
16. In-Store	Y	Y	Y	N	Y	Y	Y	Y	Y	Y
17. Gift Package	Y	Y	Y	Y	N	Y	Y	Y	P	Y
D. OFF-PACK										
18. Premium	N	N	N	P	N	Y	N	Y	P	P
19. Trading Stamps	Y	Y	Y	P	Y	Y	N	P	N	Y
E. PREMIUM MAIL-INS										
20. Free	N	N	N	N	N	Y	N	Y	N	Y
21. Liquidating	N	N	N	N	P	Y	N	Y	N	Y
F. REFUNDS										
22. Simple Refunds	Y	P	Y	P	N	P	Y	P	Y	Y
23. "Chance" Refunds	Y	N	N	N	N	N	N	P	N	Y
G. CONTESTS										
24. Simple Contest	Y	Y	Y	Y	N	Y	Y	Y	P	Y

TABLE A-1. Sales Promotion Techniques in Europe

Source: "Coupons, Samples and Sweepstakes," reproduced through courtesy of Benton & Bowles, Inc., International Advertising Agency.

been fully exploited in the concerned country. There is potential here for future innovation.

N indicates that this technique is either illegal or very strictly controlled, and thus rarely used.

With this very brief look at sales promotion possibilities in Europe, we hope we have made the point that if you are planning a promotion outside the United States you should consult with an expert from the target country. What we assume to be fair and legal isn't always so in other countries.

PROMOTION EVENT	Belgium	Denmark	France	Germany	Italy	Netherlands	Norway	Spain	Sweden	U.K.
H. SWEEPSTAKES										
25. Simple Mail-In	N	N	Y	Y	Y	N	N	Y	N	Y
26. Preselected Winners	P	N	P	Y	P	N	N	Y	N	Y
27. Winner-In-Every-Store	P	N	P	N	N	N	N	P	Y	Y
28. Games	Y	N	Y	N	N	Y	N	P	Y	Y
29. In-Home	Y	N	N	N	N	Y	N	Y	N	Y
2. Trade Oriented										
A. ALLOWANCES (REDUCED PRICE)										
30. Off-Invoice	Y	Y	Y	Y	Y	Y	Y	Y	Y	Y
31. Billback	Y	Y	Y	N	N	Y	Y	P	Y	Y
32. Count & Recount	Y	Y	Y	P	N	Y	Y	Y	P	Y
33. Advertising	Y	Y	Y	N	N	Y	Y	Y	Y	Y
34. Escalated	Y	Y	Y	Y	Y	Y	Y	Y	P	Y
35. Free Goods	Y	Y	Y	Y	Y	Y	Y	Y	Y	Y
B. BUYING TERMS										
36. Quantity Discount	Y	Y	Y	Y	Y	Y	Y	Y	P	Y
37. Prompt Payment Discount	Y	Y	Y	Y	P	Y	Y	Y	Y	Y
38. Delayed Billing	Y	Y	Y	Y	Y	Y	Y	Y	Y	Y
39. Consignment	Y	Y	Y	Y	N	Y	Y	Y	Y	Y
40. Returns	Y	Y	Y	Y	N	Y	Y	Y	Y	Y
C. PREMIUMS										
41. Dealer Loader	Y	P	Y	N	Y	Y	P	Y	P	Y
42. Merchandise Prizes	Y	P	Y	N	Y	Y	N	Y	P	Y
D. DISPLAYS										
43. Permanent	Y	N	Y	N	Y	Y	Y	Y	P	Y
44. Rotating	P	Y	Y	Y	N	Y	Y	Y	Y	Y
E. CONTESTS										
45. Display Contest	Y	N	Y	Y	N	Y	Y	Y	P	Y
F. SWEEPSTAKES										
46. Simple Sweepstakes	N	N	N	Y	N	N	N	Y	P	Y

Y indicates that this technique is *generally* legal (although often restricted) and fairly *regularly* used.

P indicates that this technique is basically legal, but has never been fully exploited in the concerned country. Potential for future innovation.

N indicates that this technique is either *illegal* or *very strictly controlled*, and thus rarely used. Detailed discussion will be necessary on each point.

Suppliers

Throughout this text we've suggested that you contact specialists and suppliers in various areas of sales promotion. We say that because it's almost impossible for one person to know all there is to know about every sales promotion technique. There is just too much information, and the risk is too great not to use every tool at your command. In addition, sales promotion is a very dynamic field —constantly changing and improving. You really need the best and most current advice you can get to make sure your sales promotion program works. That's why we suggest that you deal with the experts if you plan a promotion that requires specialized information.

To help you get started, on the following pages, we've listed some of the major sales promotion organizations and suppliers in various areas. This is not meant as a recommended list nor should it be considered a list of all the suppliers available. It is simply a list of companies and organizations who have long-term knowledge and experience in the field. In addition, most of them are members of the Promotion Marketing Association of America, Inc., the leading trade organization in the field.

You'll find listings for coupon redemption organizations, contest and sweepstakes suppliers, suppliers of continuity programs, fulfillment houses, sampling organizations, premium suppliers, and display and exhibit manufacturers. No doubt, you'll add others to this list as you become more involved in the field.

Coupon Redemption Organizations

American Premium Corp.
125 Walnut Street, Watertown, MA 02172
(617) 926-1800

Donnelly Marketing
1515 Summer Street, Stamford, CT 06905
(203) 348-9999

Incentive Services Inc.
3300 North Knox Avenue, Chicago, IL 60641
(312) 685-2000

Johnstons & Assoc.
517 East Crosstown Pkwy., Kalamazoo, MI 49001
(616) 345-0131

Marketing Services Group/Creative Display Inc.
230 E. Ohio Street, Chicago, IL 60611
(312) 642-8212

Nielsen Clearing House
1900 North Third Ave., Clinton, IA 52732
(319) 242-4505

H. Olsen & Co.
4332 North Kedzie Ave., Chicago, IL 60618
(312) 583-9696

Premium Corp. of America
12755 State Highway 55, Minneapolis, MN 55441
(612) 540-5000

Promotion & Merchandising Inc.
6734 Jimmy Carter Blvd., Norcross, GA 30071
(404) 449-6018

Spotts International
1300 Highway 3, St. Paul, MN 55112
(612) 633-3700

Stratmar Systems
385 Madison Ave., New York, NY 10017
(212) 838-1155

Contest and Sweepstakes Suppliers

Action Marketing Ltd.
580 Sylvan Ave., Englewood Cliffs, NJ 07632
(201) 569-9100

Don Jagoda Assoc.
800 Shames Drive, Westbury, NY 11590
(212) 895-4220

Marden-Kane, Inc.
666 Fifth Ave., New York, NY 10019
(212) 582-6600

H. Olsen & Co.
4332 North Kedzie Ave., Chicago, IL 60618
(312) 583-9696

Promotion Marketing Corp.
16 Wilton Road, Westport, CT 06880
(203) 227-8478

Spotts International
1300 Highway 3, St. Paul, MN 55112
(612) 633-3700

I. M. Towers & Co.
575 Lexington Ave., New York, NY 10022
(212) 421-0850

Ventura Associates
200 Madison Avenue, New York, NY 10016
(212) 889-0707

Weston Group
60 Wilton Road, Westport, CT 06880
(203) 226-6933

Continuity Program Suppliers

Encyclopaedia Britannica
425 N. Michigan Ave., Chicago, IL 60611
(312) 321-7492

Glendinning Companies
One Glendinning Place, Westport, CT 06880
(203) 226-4711

Grosset and Dunlap
51 Madison Ave., New York, NY 10021
(212) 698-9200

Northern Electric
5224 N. Kedzie, Chicago, IL 60625
(312) 267-5100

Oneida Ltd.
Oneida, NY 13421
(315) 361-3211

Palm Beach
1290 Avenue of the Americas, New York, NY 10019
(212) 582-6820

Samsonite Corp.
11200 E. 45th Avenue, Denver, CO 80239
(303) 344-6508

Sperry & Hutchinson
330 Madison Avenue, New York, NY 10017
(212) 983-2234

Sunbeam Appliance
2001 South York Rd., Oak Brook, IL 60521
(312) 654-1900

Fulfillment Organizations

D. L. Blair
185 Great Neck Road, Great Neck, NY 11021
(516) 487-9200

John Blair & Co.
717 Fifth Ave., New York, NY 10022
(212) 980-5280

Incentive Services
3300 N. Knox Ave., Chicago, IL 60641
(312) 685-2000

K Promotions
3825 W. Green Tree Rd., Milwaukee, WI 53209
(414) 352-3450

Marden-Kane, Inc.
666 Fifth Ave., New York, NY 10019
(212) 582-6600

E. F. McDonald Incentive Co.
129 S. Ludlow Street, Dayton, OH 45402
(513) 226-5252

Premium Corp. of America
12755 State Highway 55, Minneapolis, MN 55441
(612) 540-5000

Spotts International
1300 Highway 3, St. Paul, MN 55112
(612) 633-3700

Stratmar Systems
385 Madison Ave., New York, NY 10017
(212) 838-1155

Weston Group
60 Wilton Rd., Westport, CT 06880
(203) 226-6933

Sampling Organizations

John Blair & Co.
717 Fifth Ave., New York, NY 10022
(212) 980-5280

Creative Displays Inc./Marketing Service
230 E. Ohio Street, Chicago, IL 60611
(312) 642-8212

Donnelly Marketing
1515 Summer Street, Stamford, CT 06905
(203) 348-9999

The Garber Co.
Union Street, Ashland, OH 44805
(419) 289-2660

Marketing Showcase
621 Avenue of the Americas, New York, NY 10011
(212) 255-3800

Wm. Peck Sales Co.
52 Vanderbilt Ave., New York, NY 10017
(212) 661-8383

Premium Corp. of America
12755 State Highway 55, Minneapolis, MN 55441
(612) 540-5000

Promotion Development Corp.
212 Post Road, Westport, CT 06880
(203) 226-7515

Spotts International
1300 Highway 3, St. Paul, MN 55112
(612) 633-3700

Stratmar Systems
385 Madison Ave., New York, NY 10017
(212) 838-1155

Weston Group
60 Wilton Road, Westport, CT 06880
(203) 226-6933

Premium Suppliers

American Premium Corp.
125 Walnut Street, Watertown, MA 02172
(617) 926-1800

Anchor Hocking Corp.
5th and Pierce Avenue, Lancaster, OH 43130
(614) 687-2701

Ansco Photo Optical
1555 Louis Avenue, Elk Grove, IL 60007
(312) 593-7404

Bantam Books
666 Fifth Avenue, New York, NY 10019
(212) 765-7600

Bic Pen
8145 Bryan Dairy Road, Large Pinnellas County, FL 33543
(812) 393-5451

Bulova Watch
75-20 Astoria Blvd., Jackson Hts., NY 11370
(212) 335-6000

W. Atlee Burpee
300 Park Ave., Warminster, PA 18974
(215) 674-4900

Chaseline
2 Greenwich Plaza, Greenwich, CT 06830
(203) 661-3400

Corning Glass
Houghton Park, Corning, NY 14830
(607) 974-8369

Eastman Kodak
343 State Street, Rochester, NY 14650
(716) 724-4104

Ecko Housewares
9234 W. Belmont Ave., Franklin Park, IL 60131
(312) 677-3080

Encyclopaedia Britannica
425 N. Michigan Ave., Chicago, IL 60611
(312) 321-7492

Fieldcrest Mills
60 West 40th Street, New York, NY 10018
(212) 398-9500

Hamilton Beach Co.
99 Mill Street, Waterbury, CT 06720
(203) 757-6061

Hammond Inc.
515 Valley Street, Maplewood, NJ 07040
(201) 763-6000

Impact Promotions
3000 Diamond Park Drive, Dallas, TX 75265
(214) 638-8100

Incentive Services
3300 N. Knox Ave., Chicago, IL 60611
(312) 685-2000

Don Jagoda Associates
800 Shames Drive, Westbury, NY 11590
(212) 895-4220

K Promotions
3825 West Green Tree Rd., Milwaukee, WI 53209
(414) 352-3450

Libby Glass
940 Ash Street, Toledo, OH 43693
(419) 247-2387

Manhattan Shirt
1271 Avenue of the Americas, New York, NY 10022
(212) 265-3700

Mattel Sales
5150 Rosecrans Avenue, M.S. 176, Hawthorne, CA 90250
(213) 644-5521

Mirro Corp.
P.O. Box 409, Manitowoc, WI 54220
(414) 684-4421

National Premium & Merchandising
2330 Commerce Drive., P.O. Box 247, New Berlin, WI 53151
(414) 782-1510

Northern Electric
5224 N. Kedzie Ave., Chicago, IL 60625
(312) 267-5100

H. Olsen & Co.
4332 N. Kedzie Ave., Chicago, IL
(312) 583-9696

Oneida, Ltd.
Oneida, NY 13421
(315) 361-3211

Palm Beach
1290 Avenue of the Americas, New York, NY 10022
(212) 582-6820

RCA Recorder
1133 Sixth Avenue, New York, NY 10036
(212) 598-4358

Rand McNally & Co.
10 East 53rd Street, New York, NY 10022
(212) 751-6300 Ext. 15

Rawlings Sporting Goods
2500 Crescent Drive, Broadview, IL 60153
(312) 343-0710

Regal Ware
1675 Reigle Drive, Kewaskum, WI 53040
(414) 626-2121

Samsonite Corp.
11200 E. 45th Avenue, Denver, CO 80239
(303) 344-6508

Simon & Schuster
1230 Avenue of the Americas, New York, NY 10020
(212) 245-6400

Sony Corp.
9 West 57th Street New York, NY 10019
(212) 371-5800

Spaulding
7 Kilmer Road, Edison, NJ 08817
(201) 572-3184

Spotts International
1300 Highway 3, St. Paul, MN 55112
(612) 633-3700

Sunbeam Appliance
2001 S. York Road, Oak Brook, IL 60521
(312) 654-1900

Timex
P.O. Box 2126, Waterbury, CT 06720
(203) 573-5998

Travellers Premium Co.
110 Fifth Avenue, New York, NY 10011
(212) 924-1500

Van Heusen
1290 Avenue of the Americas, New York, NY 10019
(212) 541-5200

Van Schaack Premium Corp.
111 North Canal Street, Chicago, IL 60606
(312) 236-7730

Wear-Ever Aluminum
1980 Eastern Avenue, Chillicothe, OH 45601
(614) 775-9100

West Bend
400 Washington Street, West Bend, WI 53095
(414) 334-2311

Weston Group
60 Wilton Road, Westport, CT 06880
(203) 226-6933

Wham-O Manufacturing
835 E. Monte Street, San Gabriel, CA
(213) 287-9681

Whirlpool
U.S. 33 North, Administration Center, Benton Harbor, MI 49022
(616) 926-3254

Wilson Sporting Goods
2233 West Street, River Grove, IL 60171
(312) 456-6100

Display & Exhibit Manufacturers

Hall-Erickson Inc.
7237 Lake Street, River Forest, IL 60305
(312) 366-1733

Hopkins & Assoc.
8700 King Drive, Dallas, TX 75235
(214) 637-1477

Omnicom
1645 East Carboy Road, Arlington Heights, IL 60005
(312) 981-0808

Thalheim Expositions
98 Cutter Mill Road, Great Neck, NY 11021
(212) 357-3555

Index